Cricket

Cricket

Boosting Physical and Mental Well-being

Rafeal Mechlore

Leader Enterprises

CONTENTS

INDEX

Introduction

INTRODUCTION

With its grace, strategy, and friendship, cricket is a game that has captivated millions of people worldwide and has stood the test of time and geography. Cricket is not simply a game; it is a life-changing experience that touches every aspect of human existence, even though it is frequently praised for its exciting contests and amazing talent displays. In this investigation, we delve into the core of cricket's significant influence on mental and physical health, uncovering the remarkable potential of this activity to improve our overall well-being.

Outside the boundaries of a cricket ground, both fans and participants recognize the special relationship that exists between the game and living a more balanced and healthy lifestyle. Cricket symbolizes much more than just competition; it reflects a philosophy of well-being, bringing body and mind together in a perfect symphony. This is evident everywhere from the grand platforms of international stadiums to the emerald grounds of a village cricket pitch.

The goal of this book, "Cricket: Boosting Physical and Mental Well-Being," is to uncover the various ways that cricket improves our lives through an extensive trip. It looks at the ways that playing cricket improves cardiovascular health, weight control, strength, agility, and hand-eye coordination. Beyond the field of athletics, cricket promotes mental calmness, stress alleviation, and the development of strong interpersonal bonds through cooperation. It develops resilience that goes beyond the boundaries by teaching us how to concentrate under duress, make choices, and assume leadership responsibilities. In addition, the sport serves as a therapeutic instrument for improved self-esteem and personal growth, offering consolation and support to individuals dealing with mental health issues. In addition to shattering gender preconceptions, cricket has encouraged women and girls to take up the sport and advance gender equality both off the field and in society at large.

Cricket is a welcome oasis of balance in this day and age of nonstop activity, where the pressures and stressors of contemporary life can have a negative impact on our physical and mental health. It instills in us the importance of community, diversity, and unity. Cricket provides a platform for people of all ages, genders, and backgrounds to embrace the physical demands, strategic complexities, and cerebral rewards of the game while creating enduring relationships with teammates and other aficionados.

This book's voyage through its pages is not merely an ode to cricket; rather, it is an exploration of the game's capacity to change people's lives.

We will delve into the rules, gear, and strategies that make the game so fascinating as we examine the history of cricket, from its modest beginnings to its current position as a worldwide sensation. We'll hear moving tales from people whose cricket involvement has transformed their lives, and we'll learn more about the ways that cricket clubs, coaches, and mentors foster the development of a welcoming and supportive cricket community.

This book offers proof of cricket's enduring attraction and ability to improve both mental and physical health. Whether you are an experienced cricket player or thinking about picking up the game for the first time, the information and viewpoints provided here will encourage you to embrace cricket's life-changing potential. It's an invitation to experience the beauty of a sport that has been enhancing people's physical and mental health for centuries, whether you want to play on the field or just watch from the sidelines. Let's remember that cricket is more than simply a game as we set out on our journey—rather, it's a route to a happier, better, and more balanced existence.

1. **Overview of cricket as a sport**

    Known as the "gentleman's game," cricket is a popular sport with a large international fan base and a long history. It has a devoted following, a variety of media, and a sophisticated strategy. This introduction explores the history, several formats, laws, gear, and cricket's lasting appeal across the globe.

    The History of Cricket:

    The history of cricket begins in 16th-century England, when it was a popular rural past time. It developed into a recognized sport throughout time, mostly in England. The Marylebone Cricket Club (MCC), which was founded in 1787 and had a significant influence in the creation of the game's rules and regulations, was crucial in the development of cricket from the first game ever documented in the 16th century. Through colonization, cricket quickly spread to other regions of the British Empire.

    Cricket formats:

    Test Cricket: Played over five days, test cricket is the oldest and longest version of the game. The team with the most runs wins after two innings of batting for each team. Test cricket is renowned for its strategic depth, demanding a high level of talent, stamina, and focus. It's frequently regarded as the peak of the sport.

    One Day Internationals (ODIs): An ODI is a limited-overs cricket match in which two teams play one 50-over inning. This format, which was created to make cricket more widely available, has become extremely well-liked, especially in nations like England, Australia, and India.

Twenty20 (T20): With 20 overs per side, T20 cricket is the shortest format. With an emphasis on aggressive hitting, creative fielding, and exciting games, it has completely changed the sport. Two well-known T20 competitions that have increased the popularity of the format are the Indian Premier League (IPL) and the Big Bash League (BBL).

Other Formats: In addition to these primary formats, there are other variants of cricket, including List A matches and domestic Twenty20 leagues like the Caribbean Premier League (CPL) and Pakistan Super League (PSL). These genres serve a variety of audiences and are essential for developing talent.

Cricket Scoring and Rules:

When batting, a player's goal is to hit the ball that the bowler delivers in order to score runs. Running between the wickets or scoring boundaries (four or six runs in a single shot) are two ways they can score runs.

In bowling, bowlers attempt to get out batters in order to dismiss them. Getting bowled, caught, run out, or leg before wicket (LBW) are common ways to be dismissed.

Fielding: By capturing the ball or forcing a run-out, fielders hope to stop runs from being scored and remove hitters.

Overs: An over is made up of one bowler bowling from one end of the pitch for a certain number of deliveries, usually six.

Umpires: Umpires oversee the game, signaling limits, deciding on appeals, and guaranteeing fair play.

Runs are scored by a combination of running between wickets, boundaries, and penalty runs. Bowling metrics, like economy rates and wickets taken, are also critical in assessing a player's effectiveness.

Tools for Playing Cricket:

Bat: Although they exist in a variety of sizes and forms, bats have to follow the measurements given in the regulations.

Ball: Hard cork cores are found within leather cricket balls. There are various formats for using red and white balls.

Bails are little wooden pieces that rest on top of the stumps, whereas stumps are three vertical wooden posts. They make up the wicket.

Protective Gear: In order to reduce the danger of injury, players wear protective gear such as helmets, gloves, thigh guards, chest guards, and boxes (groin protection).

Dressing: Depending on the format, players wear white or colorful apparel. Cricket shoes offer traction on the pitch.

Fielding Equipment: Depending on their location on the field, fielders wear different kinds of gloves, pads, and helmets.

Popularity and Worldwide Presence:

India: With a passionate fan base, cricket is practically a religion there. One of the most popular cricket leagues in the world, the Indian Premier League (IPL) features elite players and international celebrities.

England: Known as the home of cricket, this country has a fervent fan base and holds some of the sport's most esteemed tournaments.

Australia: Legendary players and teams have come from this nation, which has a strong cultural connection to cricket.

Pakistan: Famous cricket players like Wasim Akram and Imran Khan have come from Pakistan, a nation that takes great pride in its cricket heritage.

West Indies: The West Indies, a collection of Caribbean countries, are home to some of the most thrilling and colorful cricket players in history and have a rich cricketing heritage.

World-class cricket players have been developed by committed cricketing communities in South Africa, New Zealand, and Sri Lanka.

Emerging Nations: As these nations make their impact on the global arena, cricket is becoming more popular in places like Afghanistan, Ireland, and Nepal. The International Cricket Council (ICC) is the authority that regulates cricket and is in charge of the major events and the sport's international growth. ICC World Twenty20, ICC World Test Championship, and ICC Cricket World Cup are a few of the premier tournaments that draw interest from all around the world.

Using cricket as a Uniting Factor

Cricket has a special power to bring people together from different backgrounds, tongues, and locations. It unites and strengthens the sense of pride among followers across national and political divides. Particularly amongst historically volatile nations like India and Pakistan, the sport has been crucial in advancing diplomacy and peace. These two nations have a fierce rivalry when it comes to cricket, and their matches provide diplomatic chances to foster friendship.

The Cricket Spirit:

Sportsmanship and fair play are highly valued in cricket, as embodied by the "Spirit of Cricket." Values like honesty, integrity, and respect are emphasized in this code of conduct, which is frequently credited to the renowned cricket player Sir Colin Cowdrey. It promotes respect for opponents, acceptance of umpire rulings, and adherence to the rules of the game.

The custom of recognizing athletes for their outstanding accomplishments, irrespective of the team they play for, is another way that the Spirit of Cricket is exhibited. It serves as a reminder that cricket is a celebration of the game as much as a contest of skill.

Notable Cricket Players and Their Influence:

Sir Don Bradman (Australia): Bradman, who is widely considered as the best batsman in cricket history, holds the record with a batting average of 99.94 in

Test cricket.

Indian cricketer Sachin Tendulkar, nicknamed the "Little Master," is the owner of multiple records, including the most runs in both Test and ODI matches. In India and around the world, he is a legend.

Sir Vivian Richards (West Indies): During the dominating era of the 1970s and 1980s, Richards, an aggressive and courageous batsman, was instrumental.

Garfield Sobers, a West Indian, said: As a batsman, bowler, and fielder, Sobers is regarded as one of the best all-around players in the sport's history.

New Zealander Sir Richard Hadlee: Hadlee was a vital player in the history of cricket in New Zealand and a productive fast bowler.

Imran Khan (Pakistan): Imran Khan became a well-known political figure in Pakistan after leading his country to its first-ever Cricket World Cup triumph.

Brian Lara (West Indies) was a fashionable and flashy batsman who held the record for the greatest individual Test score (400*).

Australian spin bowler Shane Warne is renowned for having had a significant influence on the game and is regarded as one of the all-time greats.

Muttiah Muralitharan (Sri Lanka): A legendary spin bowler, Muralitharan has the record for most wickets in both Test and ODI cricket.

In addition to their own accomplishments, these cricket players have served as an inspiration to countless numbers of players and fans across the globe.

Obstacles and Changing Patterns:

Commercialization: There is a widening gap between elite and grassroots cricket as a result of the emergence of T20 leagues and the sport's commercialization. It's difficult to maintain the purity of the sport while balancing financial gain.

Player Workload: With cricket players now competing in several leagues and formats, player workload and burnout are issues. Maintaining the health and fitness of players is essential.

Corruption and Match-Fixing: Integrity concerns have arisen as a result of match-fixing, spot-fixing, and corruption in cricket. To tackle these problems, anti-corruption initiatives and vigilante tactics are in place.

Diversity: The sport is working to broaden its playing base, attract new spectators, and make itself more welcoming. Women's cricket has becoming more popular, and programs such as the Global Development Program are designed to help developing cricketing nations.

Technology and Innovation: With the launch of the Decision Review System (DRS) and advancements like Hawk-Eye to increase the precision of umpiring judgments, cricket is still embracing technology.

Cricket is a sport that blends creativity with tradition, talent and strategy, passion and teamwork. Because of its historical origins in England, the game has become a worldwide phenomenon, enjoyed by people in many other countries.

Cricket has the ability to unite people, inculcate sportsmanship ideals, and produce heroes who motivate millions. Cricket continues to be a popular and enduring sport that appeals to people of all backgrounds, despite its difficulties. The sport's legacy and spirit are as strong as ever even as it continues to change and adapt to the needs of the contemporary world.

2. **The dual impact of cricket on physical and mental well-being**

The game of cricket, which is known for its strategic and intricate aspects, has a double effect on people's physical and mental health. This essay explores cricket's significant benefits for mental health, including lessons in self-discipline, teamwork, and resilience, as well as its role in enhancing physical health by encouraging athleticism and fitness. Cricket is a physical and mental sport, and it has the ability to greatly improve people's quality of life in general.

Health and Wellness:

Strength and stamina:

Cricket is a very physical sport, thus players need to be in peak physical shape. Long matches need players to possess a high degree of fitness and stamina, particularly in Test cricket. While batsmen need to have the endurance to spend hours at the crease, bowlers need to produce significant power and remain consistent over extended periods of time. In order to chase and stop balls, fielders must also be nimble and fast. Frequent cricket practice and games enhance muscular strength, endurance overall, and cardiovascular fitness.

Eye-Hand Coordination:

In cricket, batting and fielding require remarkable hand-eye synchronization. Fielders need to make accurate catches and throws, and batsmen need to respond fast to pitches with different spin and pace. Hand-eye coordination is always being improved, which improves fine motor abilities and reflexes, which can be applied in more practical ways to daily life.

Power and Adaptability:

There are many different types of movements used in cricket, such as running, sprinting, jumping, and throwing. Muscle strength and flexibility are developed as a result of this extensive physical activity. Strength of the bowling arm is especially important for bowlers as it allows them to deliver the ball accurately and quickly. Increasing flexibility and strength can help lower the chance of injury and enhance general physical well-being.

Maintaining Weight:

Regularly participating in cricket-related activities, such practise and games, can help with weight management. Players can keep a healthy body weight by combining exercise with a balanced diet. A fun and interesting method to stay active and lower your risk of obesity-related health problems is to play cricket.

Bone Thickness:

Cricket is especially good for kids and young people since it can increase bone density through weight-bearing exercises like running and sprinting. Osteoporosis and fractures later in life can be avoided by developing strong bones early in life. Regular cricket play can support bone health in the long run.

Emotional Wellness:

Resolve and Concentrate:

Playing cricket demands a great deal of focus and discipline. While bowlers must constantly maintain their line and length, batsmen must remain focused on the ball and respond fast. This degree of focus translates to everyday life, improving one's capacity to focus on assignments, establish objectives, and maintain self-discipline in the pursuit of them.

Fortitude:

Cricket players learn the value of resilience from the game's many obstacles and uncertainties. It can be mentally exhausting to face a difficult bowling attack or to try to make progress as a bowler. One of the most important life lessons is learning how to overcome setbacks and failures. This skill helps people become resilient and learn how to deal with hardship.

Collaboration and Interaction:

As a team sport, cricket depends on efficient communication and cooperation. In order to strategize, act quickly, and adjust to changing circumstances, players must cooperate. These communication and teamwork abilities translate to relationships, social situations, and the workplace, where the capacity to collaborate with others is essential.

Stress Reduction:

For some people, playing cricket can be a stress relief. Exercise releases endorphins, which have been shown to elevate mood and lower stress levels. Playing sports provides a release for tension and annoyance, enhancing mental health.

Establishing Objectives:

In cricket, players have individual and collective aims. Goal-setting is essential to the sport, whether it's accomplishing an individual objective like hitting a century or a group one like winning a competition. Setting and achieving goals is a process that may be applied to many facets of life, resulting in accomplishment and personal development.

Time Handling:

Cricket players must efficiently manage their time because the games are frequently lengthy. Competing in cricket while juggling other responsibilities like job or school helps people learn time management techniques. People who are good at managing their time can achieve success in other aspects of their lives as well as in cricket.

Controlling Emotions:

A variety of feelings can be evoked by cricket, ranging from the excitement of achievement to the dejection of defeat. It's essential for mental health to learn how to control these feelings. Cricket gives people a platform to comprehend and regulate their emotional reactions, a skill that can be very useful in a variety of real-world scenarios.

The Confluence of Mental and Physical Health:

Assurance:

A cricket player's confidence is bolstered by success, whether it's winning a match or contributing to the team's victory. This increased confidence can be applied to other facets of life, encouraging people to take on obstacles and have faith in their own skills.

Self-Regard:

Developing one's talents and playing cricket can boost one's self-esteem. A stronger sense of self-worth and self-image can result from a sense of sporting achievement, and this can have a good effect on one's self-esteem even off the cricket field.

Social Networks:

Cricket encourages a sense of community and social interaction. Friendships grow between teammates, and the cricket community provides a network of support. Cricket offers a means for people to connect with like-minded people, and social interactions and connections are crucial for mental health.

Choosing a Healthier Lifestyle:

Playing cricket frequently encourages good lifestyle decisions, like consistent exercise, a balanced diet, and enough sleep. By lowering the likelihood of stress and mood disorders, these decisions improve mental health in addition to physical health.

Optimal Mind-Body Balance:

Players are encouraged to understand the connection between their mental and physical well-being because cricket places a strong emphasis on both mental and physical components. Players can maximize their athletic ability by developing self-control over their thoughts and emotions.

The positive effects cricket has on both mental and physical health demonstrate the all-around advantages of the activity. Cricket provides a complete package of physical fitness, mental toughness, teamwork, and personal development beyond its competitive aspect. People who play this sport discover that the mental and physical components are closely linked, improving their lives both on and off the field. Cricket is more than simply a game; it's a tool for personal growth, providing lessons that help people become stronger, more resilient, and more complete people. Regardless of experience level, cricket offers a pathway for development and self-enhancement, promoting well-being in its widest sense.

3. **Purpose and scope of the book**

The key components that constitute a book's essence and mission are its purpose and scope. It is important for both authors and readers to comprehend the motivation for a book's writing as well as the boundaries it establishes regarding subject matter and viewpoint. We will analyze the idea of a book's goal and scope in this investigation, exploring their importance and the ways in which they influence the production and reception of literary works.

What a Book Is For:

Inform and Educate: The goal of writing a lot of books is to give readers knowledge and information. These could be scholarly textbooks, self-help manuals, or nonfiction publications that go deeply into a particular topic. Here, the author hopes to inform, enlighten, or raise awareness.

Entertain and Engage: The main goals of fiction writing, which includes novels, poems, and short stories, is to captivate and amuse readers. Writers may aim to take readers to new places, arouse feelings, or provide stories that will make them stop and think.

Persuade and Advocate: Writers frequently utilize their works to promote a specific cause, concept, or viewpoint. The purpose of these novels is to influence readers to take a particular stand or do something. Opinion pieces, advocacy material, and political manifestos frequently have this goal in mind.

Record and Preserve: The goal of memoirs, autobiographies, and historical narratives is to document and preserve tales, events, and experiences that are either personal or historical. Writers may choose to write in order to preserve their stories for upcoming generations.

Inspire and Motivate: The goal of several novels is to encourage and uplift their audience. These self-help or motivational books seek to offer direction and encouragement, motivating readers to make positive changes in their life, make objectives, and conquer obstacles.

Entertain and Distract: Lite fiction and popular literature frequently seek to amuse and provide a means of escape, enabling readers to temporarily forget about the difficulties of reality and lose themselves in an engrossing narrative.

Document and Research: The goal of research books and academic publications is to record research findings and add to the corpus of knowledge in a specific topic. These publications are frequently important resources for academics and learners.

Challenge and Question: Some works are published with the goal of raising issues with

accepted beliefs, casting doubt on accepted practices, or encouraging critical thought. They might try to start conversations and elicit thoughtful responses to significant problems.

A book's purpose serves as the author's beacon of guidance and inspiration as they pen their work. It is the motivation behind an author's endless hours spent composing sentences and narratives at the keyboard. In addition, the objective helps readers grasp the book's intent and what they might anticipate learning from reading it by acting as a guide.

The Book's Scope:

On the other hand, a book's scope establishes the parameters of the topics and subjects it covers. The scope establishes the parameters that will guide the author's topic exploration, analysis, and discussion. Readers should be aware of a book's scope in order to properly assess the breadth and depth of its content.

The scope may include various important elements:

Subject Matter: The book's primary theme or topic is defined by its subject matter. It outlines the subject matter of the book and offers a structure for its contents. A historical fiction, for instance, can concentrate on a particular era or occasion.

Geographic or Temporal Restrictions: The scope of certain works is limited by geographic or temporal restrictions. For example, a historical account may concentrate on a specific time period, area, or series of events.

Depth of Analysis: The author's level of exploration into a certain topic is also determined by the scope. While some books give a thorough introduction to a subject, others offer specialized, in-depth assessments.

Target Audience: The size of a book is largely determined by its intended readership. A popular scientific book may seek to reach a wider audience, whereas an academic textbook may have a narrow focus and be designed for students in a particular discipline.

Interdisciplinary Considerations: A book may occasionally incorporate ideas from different fields or viewpoints, broadening its focus to offer a more complete picture of the topic.

A book's scope greatly influences its substance and organization. It keeps writers on task and keeps them from wandering off into irrelevant areas. It is essential for readers to comprehend the breadth in order to set reasonable expectations and choose books that suit their requirements and interests.

The Relationship between Scope and Purpose:

A book's goal and its scope are closely related. The aim of the author determines the scope by dictating the features of the subject matter that will be examined and to what extent. Together, these two components produce a literary work that is both coherent and significant.

A book on a particular historical event, for instance, would probably have a scope that includes a thorough analysis of the event's causes, effects, and historical background. The scope outlines the parameters within which the author will impart knowledge to the reader, while the purpose instructs the writer on how to do so.

Similarly, the scope may include the characters, storyline, and locations that support the captivating narrative if the goal is to entertain and engage, as is frequently the case with novels. The scope describes the narrative universe in which the author intends to entertain. The author's goal is to amuse.

Nonetheless, there are situations in which the scope and goal might not coincide exactly. Even though the author's goal is to educate readers about history, there are times when word count or research availability force the author to focus just on a single event or era of history. In these cases, the scope acts as a useful restriction, while the purpose gives the overall objective.

A book's ability to effectively accomplish its goals ultimately rests on how well its scope and purpose mesh. When these two factors are in harmony, readers may expect a well-rounded and satisfying reading experience that is consistent with the author's goals.

Obstacles & Things to Think About:

Clarity: To make sure that readers know what to expect, the goal and scope should be made explicit. In these situations, ambiguity might result in misinterpretations and disgruntled readers.

Balance: It's crucial to strike the correct balance between the goals and reach of a book. Scopes that are too wide or too narrow might not be in line with the goal.

Adaptability: As they get deeper into the writing process, authors should be willing to change the scope. The scope of the book may occasionally need to be revised as a result of the research or creative process.

Reader-Centric Approach: When defining the goal and parameters of a book, authors should take their target audience's wants and interests into account. This focus on the reader can increase the book's significance and influence.

Ethical Considerations: Writers should be aware of ethical issues while crafting persuasive or advocacy writing, making sure that their message is responsible and considerate of other viewpoints.

A book's aim and purview act as the compass points that determine its purpose and the limits of its investigation. These components are inextricably intertwined and combine to produce a literary work that both satisfies readers' needs and accomplishes the author's goals. For writers as well as readers, knowing the goal and scope of a book is essential since it offers a path for creation and sets expectations for consumption. In order for readers to choose books that suit their interests, needs, and curiosities, authors must make sure that the aim and scope of their literary works are clearly specified.

4. **The significance of promoting well-being through sports**

Everyone aspires to be happy, and participating in sports is a great way to reach this objective. Sports and physical activity play a critical role in improving mental, emotional, and social well-being in addition to improving physical health. This essay examines the enormous importance of using sports to promote wellbeing and touches on the many advantages it has for both individuals and society.

Health and Wellness:
Enhanced Physical Health:
A readily obvious advantage of engaging in sports is enhanced physical fitness. Engaging in regular physical activity improves cardiovascular health, strength, endurance, and helps people maintain a healthy body weight. A variety of activities, including basketball and soccer, swimming, and jogging, provide opportunities to maintain physical fitness.

Lower Chance of Chronic Illnesses:
Playing sports lowers the risk of obesity, heart disease, diabetes, and hypertension, among other chronic diseases, greatly. Participating in sports helps lower cholesterol, regulate weight, and improve metabolic health in general.

Improved Motor Abilities:
Complex motions found in sports call for agility, balance, and coordination. People's motor abilities are improved, and it helps them keep their physical dexterity throughout their life.

Robust joints and bones
Weight bearing is a vital component of many sports and is essential for bone health. Playing sports helps build stronger bones, which lowers the chance of osteoporosis and fractures in later life.

Emotional Wellness:
Reduced Stress:
Participating in sports is a great way to relieve stress. Naturally occurring mood enhancers called endorphins are released when one engages in physical activity. Playing sports promotes mental health by assisting people in reducing stress and anxiety.

Better Mental Well-Being:
There are numerous advantages of sports for mental health. Frequent exercise can improve general mental resilience, increase self-esteem, and lessen the symptoms of anxiety and depression. The social component of team sports also aids in preventing feelings of loneliness.

Mental Process:
Sports and other forms of physical activity have been related to enhanced cognitive performance. It improves focus, memory, and problem-solving skills. This is especially advantageous for young children and teenagers who are still developing.

Goal-setting and Self-Control:
Playing sports teaches perseverance, goal-setting, and self-discipline. Athletes acquire goal-setting skills, rigorous work ethic, and a strong feeling of resolve that they may use in a variety of real-world scenarios.

Emotional Health:
Increased Self-Respect:

Reaching personal goals and having athletic achievement are two ways to increase self-esteem. This favorable self-perception can boost people's confidence and sense of value outside of the sports arena and into everyday life.

Relationship with Others:

Playing sports frequently fosters social contact, teamwork, and togetherness. A sense of community and emotional support can result from establishing and sustaining relationships through sports. For kids and teenagers in particular, this is crucial as they develop social ties.

Pleasure and Laughter:

Sports are by their very nature joyful activities that provide people the chance to relax, enjoy themselves, and feel joy. Playing sports has a positive emotional impact, which plays a significant role in fostering general contentment and happiness.

Emotional Health:

Building Communities:

Communities can come together through sports. Local sports teams, gatherings, and competitions encourage a feeling of pride in the community and advance social well-being. They offer a forum for social interaction, mutual support, and celebration of accomplishments.

Cultural Interaction:

International sporting events, like the Olympics or the FIFA World Cup, present a special chance for diplomatic and cultural interchange. These international gatherings break down social and political barriers by bringing nations together in a spirit of collaboration and competition.

Diversity and Inclusivity:

Sports encourage diversity and inclusivity by giving participants of all ages, skills, and backgrounds the chance to participate. This promotes social integration and values personal uniqueness.

In charge and accountable:

Athletics may foster a sense of accountability and leadership. In their communities, athletes

frequently act as role models, encouraging people to participate in sports and live up to moral principles.

Sports have a big role in promoting wellbeing for both individuals and society. Participating in sports has a direct impact on one's social, mental, emotional, and physical health. Sports have a positive effect on communities as a whole and strengthen social links, in addition to having an individual influence.

Societies can endeavor to create inclusive and accessible sporting settings that enable individuals of all ages and backgrounds to take advantage of the many benefits that sports have to offer as long as they continue to acknowledge the fundamental relevance of sports in promoting well-being. Sports may play a major role in promoting well-being, and by doing so, communities can become more lively, happier, and healthier.

Chapter 1

The Basics of Cricket

With a rich history and a large international fan base, cricket is a sport with complex regulations, many formats, and ardent supporters. This thorough introduction to the fundamentals of cricket explores the history of the game, its core principles, the gear used on the field, player positions, and the subtleties of hitting, bowling, and fielding. It also examines the many forms of cricket, such as Twenty20 (T20) cricket, One Day Internationals (ODIs), and Test matches, giving readers a comprehensive grasp of this cherished sport.

Cricket's beginnings and evolution:

The history of cricket begins in 16th-century England, when it was a popular rural past time. It developed into a recognized sport throughout time, mostly in England. The Marylebone Cricket Club (MCC), which was founded in 1787 and had a significant influence in the creation of the game's rules and regulations, was crucial in the development of cricket from the first game ever documented in the 16th century. Through colonization, cricket quickly made its way to other regions of the British Empire, influencing nations like Australia, India, and the West Indies.

Basic Guidelines for Play:

Goal of the Match:

In cricket, the main goal is for one side to score more runs than the other. Teams alternate between bowling and batting, with the bowling team trying to restrict scoring and dismiss batters while the batting team seeks to score as many runs as they can.

Innards:

The term "inning" describes a team's batting turn. In a typical match, two innings are given to each team, one after the other. The bowling team looks to take wickets and limit the opposition's scoring while the batting team aims to score runs during their innings.

Scores and Runs:

By striking the ball and sprinting between the wickets, batsmen can score runs. Aside from scoring runs by striking boundaries, they can also score six runs for clearing the boundary without the ball bouncing and four runs for striking the ball on the boundary rope.

Dismissals and Wickets:

Getting a batsman out, often known as "taking their wicket," is the main way to remove someone from the game. The following are common ways to be dismissed: bowled (ball hitting the stumps and removing the bails), caught (ball being caught by a fielder before it hits the ground), and leg before wicket (LBW) (ball hitting the stumps but being blocked by the batsman's leg). Stumped, hit wicket, and run out are some other ways to be dismissed.

Judges and Making Decisions:

Umpires supervise games, deciding on appeals, indicating boundaries, and guaranteeing fair play. They work together to reach conclusions, and in competitive matches, tools like the Decision Review System (DRS) are utilized to help in decision-making in specific circumstances.

Plaything Supplies:

Ball of cricket:

Typically, a leather casing covers a cork cricket ball that has been wrapped in twine. Traditionally, it is white for limited-overs cricket and red for Test cricket.

Baseball Bat:

The cricket bat has a cane grip and a flat blade made of willow wood. The cricket authorities have set some rules regarding its weight and dimensions.

Bails and Stumps:

Three vertical wooden posts called stumps are positioned at each end of the field. Little wooden pieces called bails are placed atop the stumps and, when removed, represent a dismissal.

Safety Equipment:

To reduce the danger of injury, cricket players use a variety of protective gear, such as helmets, gloves, thigh guards, chest guards, leg guards (pads), and boxes (groin protection).

Cricket Apparel:

Traditionally, cricketers have worn white or cream-colored apparel, particularly during Test matches. Depending on the tournament regulations, colored apparel may be permitted in limited-overs formats.

Roles and Positions of Players:

Man-bats:

The batting team is in charge of scoring runs. At any given time, there are two batsmen on the field who collaborate to score runs and defend their wickets from the bowlers.

Players of bowling:

With the intention of getting the batsmen out, bowlers deliver the ball to them. Fast bowlers, spin bowlers, and medium-pace bowlers are among the several kinds of bowlers, and they all have unique methods and approaches.

Wicket Man:

A specialist fielder, the wicketkeeper stands behind the wicket to try run-outs, stumpings, and catches off the bowler's deliveries in addition to collecting balls that the batsman has not hit.

Observers:

In order to stop runs from being scored and to remove hitters from the game, fielders are essential. In accordance with the bowler's strategies and the batsman's playing style, they are positioned strategically all around the field.

Cricket formats:

Test match chess:

The longest format is test cricket, which is played over five days with two innings each team. It is renowned for its strategic nuance and endurance, and is frequently regarded as the pinnacle of a player's ability and endurance tests.

International One-Day Events (ODIs):

ODIs are limited-overs games in which 50 overs are played in a single inning by each team. They provide a nice counterpoint to the fast-moving intensity of Twenty20 matches and the strategic difficulties of Test cricket.

Twenty20 Cricket (T20):

The shortest format in cricket is T20, with 20 overs each side. Because it places a strong emphasis on aggressive batting, creative fielding, and high-scoring games, it is well-liked by time-pressed viewers.

National Leagues:

Many nations have their own domestic leagues, like the Big Bash League (BBL) and the Indian Premier League (IPL), which draw elite international players and provide local talent a chance to show off their abilities.

Major Events and Cricket Tournaments:

ICC Competitions:

Teams from all over the world fight for the top spot in international cricket at the International Cricket Council's (ICC) major competitions, which include the ICC Champions Trophy, ICC World Twenty20, and ICC Cricket World Cup.

Series of Ashes:

The Ashes is an important sports and historical series of Test cricket played every two years between Australia and England. The series, which has been a mainstay of the cricket calendar for more than a century, is renowned for its fierce rivalries.

Other Important Competitions:

A number of other significant competitions, like the Asia Cup, Pakistan Super League (PSL), and Caribbean Premier League (CPL), highlight the skill of players from certain areas and allow them a chance to participate at a high level.

Cricket is a global sport that has captured the hearts of millions of people due to its rich history, complex regulations, and variety of formats. Cricket has come a long way from its humble beginnings in rural England to its current standing as a major international sport, and it still draws new participants and fans. For both aficionados and players, having a fundamental understanding of cricket's regulations, gear, player positions, and formats is essential. The game's continued growth and adaptation to the contemporary day bears witness to the unwavering competitive spirit and emotion that characterize cricket's ageless appeal.

1.1 A brief history of cricket

With a centuries-long history, cricket is a sport renowned for its rich traditions and fervent fan base. Cricket was first played in rural England and has since spread throughout the world. This in-depth history of cricket transports us back in time to examine the game's modest origins, the establishment of the first cricket clubs, its growth throughout the British Empire, and its evolution into the contemporary version that we know today.

The History of Cricket:

Cricket's precise beginnings are lost in the mists of time, but its history dates back to medieval England. The sport was first mentioned in court in 1598, when a young man by the name of John Derrick was charged with playing "cricket" on Guildford, Surrey's common ground. This was probably a simple game with a ball and a stick, an early form of cricket.

Cricket's name is thought to have come from the Old English word "cric," which meant crutch or staff. The name made sense because, at first, cricket bats were long and looked like walking poles. Stump and a wicket, consisting of two bails and one bail, were frequently used as the game progressed.

The 17th century saw the growth of cricket:

The 17th century saw the rise in popularity of cricket, especially during the English Civil War (1642–1651). It is reported that during times of idleness, soldiers from both sides engaged in this sport. Teams from Kent and London engaged in a two-day match in 1646, the earliest documented mention of a cricket match.

One of the most famous cricket venues, Lord's Cricket Ground, has been around since 1715 when the Long Room was built.

The Origin of Organized Cricket in the Eighteenth Century:

The first cricket clubs were founded in the eighteenth century, and organized cricket was born. Many people believe that the Hampshire-based Hambledon Club, which was established in 1750, was the first official cricket club. They were essential in formalizing the leg before wicket (LBW) rule and the follow-on concept, among other regulations governing the game.

The Marylebone Cricket Club (MCC), established at Lord's Cricket Ground in 1787, was instrumental in bringing the game's regulations into uniformity. The "Laws of Cricket" developed by the MCC served as the model for current cricket laws. One of the most recognizable cricket grounds in the world is still Lord's, and the MCC is still a major force in the game.

The History of Bowling and Batting:

Both batting and bowling technique improvement started to take shape in the 18th century. Bowlers experimented with a variety of bowling techniques, such as underarm, roundarm, and overarm. With the development of straight bats and the usage of hand-in-gloves, which improved control and accuracy, batting techniques also changed.

The 19th Century: First-Class Cricket's Emergence:

Cricket's history saw a dramatic shift in the 19th century. In Canada in 1785, the first-ever cricket match in North America was documented. Australia was also introduced to cricket, with the first game taking place there in 1803. But one of the most distinctive aspects of this period was the rise of first-class cricket, which is frequently considered the highest form of the game.

The All-England XI, which included the greatest cricket players at the time, was established in 1810. As it competed against different teams, competitive cricket was born. The first-ever international cricket match took place in New York in 1844 between a team of cricket players from the United States and an English squad captained by William Clarke.

An important turning point in cricket history occurred in 1846 when Australia and England played their first formal match in Melbourne, which is regarded as the beginning of Test cricket. Test cricket, played between national teams, became the official format of the game after this momentous occasion.

Cricket's Spread Throughout the British Empire:

Cricket's influence grew over the world along with the British Empire. During the 19th century, the sport was brought to South Africa, New Zealand, India, the West Indies, and other British territories. With the founding of the first cricket club in 1792 in Calcutta (now Kolkata), cricket became incredibly popular in India.

The Ashes: The Most Well-Known Rivalry in Cricket:

One of cricket's most famous rivalries, the Ashes series, originated with an obituary published in The Sporting Times in 1882. The newspaper declared, very cynically, that English cricket was dead after England's match at The Oval against Australia. It was rumored that English cricket's ashes were shipped to Australia, and a spoof obituary gave rise to the Ashes series, a representation of the two countries' ongoing rivalry. Since then, the Ashes series has grown to be one of the sport's most beloved competitions.

The Introduction of Twenty-Over Cricket:

The 20th century saw cricket continue to develop. The first official One Day International (ODI) was played in Melbourne in 1971 between Australia and England. With only 60 overs each side, the format provided a quicker and more approachable version of the game. ODIs gained enormous popularity, and the inaugural Cricket World Cup took place in 1975.

Twenty20 (T20) Cricket's Ascent:

Twenty20 (T20) cricket is a fast-growing cricket format that has become popular in the twenty-first century. Matches are short, high-scoring affairs that last about three hours. The Indian Premier League (IPL) and the Big Bash League (BBL) are two local T20 competitions that have helped to further popularize the format after the first ICC World Twenty20 was staged in 2007. T20 cricket provided thrilling entertainment, drawing a larger audience and establishing itself as a global sensation.

Contemporary Cricket and Worldwide Growth:

Currently, cricket is a major international sport with large fan bases in a number of nations, including South Africa, the West Indies, Pakistan, Australia, India, and England. The International Cricket Council (ICC) oversees international cricket and hosts a number of competitions, such as the ICC Cricket World Cup and the ICC World Twenty20. The sport has grown beyond its historical confines.

With the use of technology, such as the Decision Review System (DRS), which uses ball-tracking and video evidence to improve the accuracy of umpiring judgments, cricket has responded to the demands of the modern day. Digital platforms have contributed to the growth of the sport's appeal by allowing spectators to follow players and matches from anywhere in the world.

The history of cricket demonstrates its enduring popularity and ability to change with the times. Cricket has come a long way from its mysterious beginnings as a country pastime to becoming a major international sport. The game is still one of the most treasured and adored in the world because of its rich traditions, legendary rivalries, and fervent fan base. Cricket is a living example of the ageless spirit of rivalry and the uniting force of sport as it develops and grows.

1.2 Cricket as a team sport

Cricket is a sport that embodies the spirit of teamwork, with its rich history and widespread appeal. Cricket is a team sport that places a strong emphasis on player cooperation, planning, and collaboration. Each player's contribution is vital to the team's success. This thorough analysis explores the nuances of cricket as a team sport, emphasizing the importance of cooperation in many areas of the game and how it affects the dynamics and performance of the team.

Working Together and Communicating:

Successful cooperation in cricket requires effective communication and collaboration. To coordinate their efforts and make wise decisions, players depend on clear and unambiguous communication throughout the game, from developing game plans to putting them into practice on the field. In order to ensure that all team members are in sync with the game strategy and equipped to adjust to changing circumstances on the field, captains and team leaders assume a critical role in promoting open communication. Coordination of batting partnerships, fielding positions, and bowling strategies are also made easier by effective communication, which empowers players to predict and strategically react to the movements of the opposition.

Positions and Accountabilities:

Like any other team sport, cricket demands that players carry out their roles and tasks in order to accomplish group goals. A unique role is given to each player according to their abilities, knowledge, and strengths. While bowlers concentrate on capturing wickets and limiting the scoring pace, batsmen are in charge of making runs and forming partnerships. In order to keep order behind the stumps and assist the bowlers in getting out, wicketkeepers are essential. As part of the team's overall defense plan, fielders place themselves strategically on the field to stop runs and make catches. A team's cohesiveness and performance are largely dependent on each member knowing their function and carrying it out well.

Planning Strategically and Making Decisions:

In cricket, successful results depend on smart decision-making and strategic planning. Teams design a strategy based on a variety of game elements, including pitch conditions, player strengths and limitations, and the opposition's style of play, in order to take advantage of the opposition's shortcomings and maximize their own advantages. When it comes to making decisions, captains and coaches are essential. They choose batting orders, fielding positions, and bowling changes. The team's performance and overall success in the game can be greatly impacted by their capacity to make wise decisions under duress.

Team cohesion and dynamics:

In cricket, a friendly and cooperative atmosphere must be fostered through positive team chemistry and cohesiveness. Cultivating a cohesive team culture that feeds on joint achievement requires cultivating a sense of camaraderie, mutual respect, and trust among team members. Activities that foster teamwork, encouraging one another, and acknowledging individual and group accomplishments all help to create a healthy work environment. A cohesive team generates a sense of togetherness and shared purpose among the players and is better able to face obstacles, overcome failures, and retain a resilient attitude.

Alliances & Partnerships:

Cricket highlights the importance of alliances and partnerships between players, especially in

the batting area. In batting partnerships, two batters cooperate with one another to withstand the opposition's bowling attack and amass a sizable run total. Effective communication, understanding, and the capacity to balance each other's playing styles are necessary for partnerships to succeed. Building solid alliances encourages trust and comradery among players, which makes it possible for them to assist one another and raise the team's score as a whole.

Flexibility and Adaptability:

Cricket teams need to develop a lot of adaptability and flexibility in order to react to shifting game dynamics and unanticipated obstacles. Based on the changing conditions of the game, including pitch behavior, weather patterns, and the performance of the opponent, teams must modify their strategies, tactics, and playing methods. Teams can stay competitive and keep an advantage over the opponent by having the flexibility to quickly adjust to unforeseen conditions and make strategic modifications in real-time.

Mentoring and Leadership:

A culture of excellence and teamwork in cricket requires strong leadership and mentoring. Within the team, new and aspiring talents are guided and nurtured by captains, coaches, and senior players who act as role models and mentors. They offer insightful commentary, impart technical expertise, and inculcate in the athletes the virtues of self-control, tenacity, and sportsmanship. Players are inspired to collaborate as a team by strong leadership and mentoring, which drives them to aim for ongoing development and group achievement.

Team Appreciations and Thoughts:

In cricket, building a positive team culture requires regular reflection on the team's performance

and celebration of accomplishments. Celebrations as a team after big achievements, such as hundreds, five-wicket hauls, or wins in a match, help players feel more accomplished and bonded. Players can evaluate their performance, pinpoint areas for development, and come up with plans for improving their general gaming and teamwork through post-match reflections and team talks. The team's learning and development are aided by these reflections, which promote a culture of ongoing development and progress.

The fundamental aspect of cricket as a team sport is its focus on player cooperation, planning, and coordination in order to attain group success. A cohesive and successful cricket team is mostly dependent on strategic planning, effective communication, well defined roles, and favorable team dynamics. Cricket teams may develop a resilient spirit, mutual trust, and a drive for greatness both on and off the field by cultivating a culture of teamwork, adaptation, and mentorship. Cricket's continuing emphasis on teamwork is a key component of the sport's ageless appeal and global history, even as it continues to evolve.

1.3 Key rules and regulations

The sport of cricket, which has a long and illustrious history and is popular all over the world, is governed by a set of rules and regulations that aim to ensure fair play, uphold the game's honor, and offer a competitive environment that is well-organized. The players, the referees, and the spectators all need to have a solid understanding of these rules. In this extensive reference, we discuss the most important laws and regulations of the sport of cricket. These rules and regulations cover a variety of areas of the game, including the playing surface, the equipment, the gameplay, and behavior both on and off the field.

The Level of Competition:

The Sell:

The cricket pitch is a rectangular space that is located in the middle of the field and is 20.12 meters (22 yards) in length. It is composed of the batting crease, the bowler's crease, and the popping crease. These are the three distinct sections.

Folds and creases:

A batsman is considered to be in a safe zone known as the crease while they are standing there facing the bowler.

Bowler's Crease refers to the area from which the bowler delivers the ball to the target.

The Popping Crease denotes the area when a batsman is in no danger while dashing between the wickets.

The Stump and the Bail:

At each end of the playing field, there are three wooden stumps set, and on top of those stumps, there are two bails. The bowler's job is to hit the stumps hard enough to knock off the bails, which will result in the batter being out of the game.

The limit is:

A field is said to have a border if there is a marked boundary line that goes all the way around it. It is regarded as a boundary when a batsman hits the ball over the boundary without it touching the ground first. This results in either four runs (grounded) or six runs (over the boundary).

The Closed Group:

In limited-overs formats, the number of fielders that can be deployed outside of this area is restricted due to the presence of an inner circle that is demarcated 30 yards from the stumps. The purpose of this regulation is to maintain a healthy equilibrium between batting and bowling.

Equipment for the Player:

Bat:

Willow wood is utilized in the construction of cricket bats, and there are strict guidelines regarding the dimensions, weight, and types of wood that can be used. In order to maintain a level playing field, bats must conform to the established standards.

Ball:

The outer layer of a cricket ball is composed of leather, and the inside is constructed of cork and twine. They are available in two colors: white for limited-overs formats and red for the traditional Test cricket format. Both the seam and the shine on the ball play an important part in deciding how it moves when it's in play.

Equipment for Self-Defense:

When batting, keeping wickets, or fielding near to the batsman, cricket players defend themselves by wearing protective gear like as helmets, leg guards (pads), gloves, thigh guards, chest guards, and boxes (groin protection). This helps to reduce the likelihood of suffering an injury.

How to Play:

The inning:

In the game of cricket, each team bats for two innings during a test match, but only bats once during other types of matches, such as those with limited overs. When all of the batsmen are out of the game, the captain can proclaim the inning over, or when the target is met, the inning is over.

Runners and Points Scored:

It is possible to score runs by either striking the boundary or running between the wickets. The batter can score four runs by hitting the ball to the boundary, and six runs by hitting the ball so far that it goes over the boundary and does not touch the ground.

Wickets and Dismissals:

The dismissal of the batters should always be the number one priority for the fielding squad. The following are common ways a batter can be removed from the game: bowled (which occurs when the ball hits the stumps), caught (which occurs when a fielder catches the ball), leg before wicket (LBW), run out, stumped, or struck wicket.

Bowling:

The objective of the bowlers is to take wickets and slow down the rate at which runs are scored

by delivering the ball to the batting team. Bowlers come in a variety of styles, including fast bowlers, spin bowlers, and medium-pace bowlers. Each of these bowlers employs a unique set of strategies.

Positions on the Fielding:

The fielding team works to cut down on runs and make catches by positioning its men in the optimal spots on the field. The bowler's strategy and the batsman's playing style both have an impact on the fielding positions that are taken.

Rules to be Followed by Bowlers:

When Compared to:

Bowlers are only allotted a certain amount of overs to bowl in each inning when the game is played using a limited-overs system. For instance, in a One-Day International (also known as an ODI), the maximum number of overs that a bowler is permitted to bowl is 10.

No-balls and wide deliveries: the game continues

When a bowler delivers a no-ball (when their foot crosses the crease as they are delivering the ball) or a wide (when the ball is delivered too far away from the batsman), they receive a penalty. These result in additional runs for the team that is batting in formats that have a limited number of overs.

Restrictions on the Field:

The fielding limits that are used in limited-overs forms, including the powerplay, stipulate that only a set number of fielders are permitted to be outside the inner circle during specific periods of the game.

Instructions for Batsmen

"LBW" stands for "Leg Before Wicket":

If the ball would have hit the stumps but the batsman's leg was in the way, then the batsman could be given out leg before wicket (LBW). When deciding whether or not a batter is out for an LBW, umpires apply very specific criteria.

Regulations for Playing the Field:

A batter cannot be purposefully hindered or distracted by a fielder's actions. There are other regulations for batsmen that govern how they can and cannot block the field.

The Run-Outs

A batsman can be removed from the game by a run-out if they are unable to return to their crease in time after the bails on the stumps have been removed by the fielding side while the batsman is outside of their crease.

Decisions Made by the Umpire:

Umpires who work on the field:

The match is officiated by two on-field umpires, who make judgments about LBW, caught behind, run-outs, and other events that occur on the field. In addition to it, they indicate boundaries, dismissals, and no-balls.

The third umpire is:

There is typically a third umpire present in international matches. This umpire employs technology, such as ball-tracking, to examine decisions, particularly those that are controversial, such as run-outs and boundary catches.

The Decision Review System, abbreviated as DRS:

The Decision Review mechanism (DRS) is a technology-driven mechanism that provides teams with the opportunity to contest the judgments made by umpires. It allows a certain number of reviews per inning to review caught-behind and LBW calls, but only a certain amount.

Standards of Ethical Conduct:

Cricket's enduring tradition:

The "Spirit of Cricket" is a code of conduct for the sport of cricket that places an emphasis on fair play, respect for opponents, and sportsmanship. It incentivizes participants to play honestly and maintain the game's standards.

Players and support staff are required to abide by the following code of conduct:

Codes of conduct have been established by cricket's governing bodies, such as the International Cricket Council (ICC), which detail the anticipated behavior of players and support staff. Fines, suspensions, and other types of punishments may be imposed in response to violations.

Tampering with the Ball:

It is definitely against the rules to change the state of the ball in any way. Any effort to alter the ball in any way, including the introduction of foreign substances, can result in serious penalties, including suspensions from the game.

The rules and regulations of cricket offer a defined framework for the game, which helps to ensure that it is played fairly, safely, and with good sportsmanship. To fully appreciate the complexities of the sport, it is essential for players, officials, and fans alike to have a solid grasp of these laws. Whether it be the dimensions of the playing field, the specifications for equipment, the laws controlling gaming, or the norms of behavior, the rules and regulations of cricket are designed to safeguard the game's integrity while yet allowing for competitive and compelling contests on the field. Cricket's ongoing popularity and its status as one of the most admired sports in the world are both due, in large part, to the regulations that govern the game.

1.4 Equipment and field layout

Cricket is a sport that is noted for its elegance and the intricacy of its strategic aspects. In order to promote fair and competitive gameplay, specific equipment and a well-defined field layout are required. In this in-depth guide, we dig into the necessary equipment that cricket players utilize, the specifics of the cricket field, and the tactical relevance of field location in the game of cricket. To fully appreciate the complexities of cricket and the game's enduring allure, it is essential to have a solid grasp of these aspects of the sport.

Equipment Used in Cricket:

Bat for Cricket:

The cricket bat is regarded as one of the most recognizable symbols associated with the sport of cricket. Willow wood, specifically either English willow or Kashmir willow, is used in its construction. Willow bats are constructed with a cane handle, a protective grip, and a blade that is flattened. Bats are available in a wide range of sizes and weights, but they must all adhere to the regulations that have been established by the cricket authorities.

Ball Used in Cricket:

Cork serves as the base of cricket balls, which are then wrapped in twine and leather to complete their construction. They are available in two colors: red and white, with the former being used for the test format of cricket and the latter being used for the limited-overs format. The seam of the ball is a very important component in determining how it will behave both in the air and when it is not in play.

The Stump and the Bail:

At either end of the cricket field, there is a set of three wooden stumps that have been hammered into the ground, and on top of those stumps are two bails. In cricket, the creases are denoted by stumps and bails, which also serve as a target for bowlers who are attempting to dismiss the batsmen.

Equipment for Self-Defense:

Helmets are worn to protect the head and face from being struck by incoming projectiles.

Leg Guards, also known as Pads, are worn when batting and fielding to protect the legs from getting hurt.

Gloves are worn so that batting and wicketkeeping do not cause injury to the hands.

Protecting the thighs from potential injury when batting is the purpose of thigh guards.

Protecting the chest area from potential harm is the primary purpose of chest guards.

Boxes, also known as groin protectors, are worn by male athletes to reduce the risk of injury to the groin region.

Equipment Used in Wicket Keeping:

Additional protective gear, such as leg guards, gloves, and a helmet with a faceguard, is worn by wicket keepers in cricket matches. Webbing is sewn in between the fingers of a wicketkeeper's gloves so that they can more easily catch the ball.

What to Wear:

White or cream is the preferred color for cricket players to wear in traditional matches, particularly Test matches. Colored apparel is permitted to be worn during limited-overs versions of cricket, such as One-Day Internationals (ODIs) and Twenty20 (T20) matches. The players dress in long pants, shirts, and individualized team jerseys when they compete.

Shoes with Spikes:

Spikes designed specifically for use in cricket are attached to the bottom of the soles of cricket shoes. Players that use spiked shoes are better able to keep their balance and avoid slipping while they compete.

Pads for the Batsman:

In addition to the protection that the leg guards provide for the batsman's legs and thighs, these pads further enhance that protection. They are especially beneficial when going up against fast bowlers.

Field Configuration:

The Business End of Cricket:

Batting Crease: The batting crease is denoted by a white line that is 1.22 meters in length and is located where the batsman stands in order to defend their wicket.

Bowler's Crease: The bowler's crease is located at the opposite end of the pitch and is denoted by a white line that is 1.22 meters in length. This is where the bowler delivers the ball.

Popping Crease: The popping crease is a more diminutive white line that is located 1.22 meters in front of the batting crease. In order to avoid being run out, batters must keep at least a portion of their body or bat behind this line.

The Stump and the Bail:

The field is set up with three stumps and two bails at each end of the playing area. The stumps are driven into the ground. The height of the stumps is 71.1 centimeters (28 inches), and there is a gap of 22.86 centimeters (9 inches) between each one of them.

The bowling and batting ends are as follows:

The end of the pitch where bowling takes place is called the bowling end, while the end where

batting takes place is called the batting end. While the bowler stands at the end designated for bowling, the batsman will be located at the end designated for batting.

Positions on the Fielding:

The bowler, batter, and format of the game all have an impact on the positions that players take on the field. When it comes to close-catching fielders, common fielding positions include silly point, slips, gully, leg slip, short leg, and short leg slip. Fielders who are patrolling different sections of the field will employ terms such as "mid-off," "mid-on," "square leg," "fine leg," "point," and "cover."

The limit is:

The playing field is surrounded by a border that may be a rope or a line that has been painted on the ground. It delineates the area beyond which a batsman's stroke is regarded a boundary, which can result in either four runs (if the ball hits the ground before clearing the boundary) or six runs (if the ball clears the boundary on the full) for the batting team.

The Closed Group:

An inner circle is drawn out at a distance of 30 yards (27.43 meters) from the stumps in limited-overs variations of the game. The presence of a specified number of fielders inside this circle during certain phases of the game is mandatory in order to maintain a healthy balance between the batting and the fielding aspects of the game.

Preparation of the Pitch:

The preparation of the cricket pitch is a labor-intensive procedure that includes rolling, mowing, and otherwise grooming the pitch in order to produce a uniform and smooth surface for the game. Because the condition of the pitch has the potential to greatly influence the way the ball moves, it is a crucial consideration in the game.

Markings on the Pitch:

The field is marked with a variety of lines and markings that help with decision-making and field placement.

These are the creases, the return crease, and the popping crease, all of which play a significant role in establishing whether or not the deliveries and run-outs in question are legitimate.

Positioning of Strategic Forces in the Field:

The positioning of the field is a crucially important strategic consideration in cricket. The playing style of the batter, the bowler's strategies, and the current condition of the match are taken into consideration while determining where to position the fielders. The following are some major fielding positions and the relevance of such positions from a strategic perspective:

Fielders who slip:

On either the leg side or the off side, next to the wicketkeeper, is where you'll find the slip fielders. They are meant to prevent the fast bowler from getting an edge off of the batsman's shot, which is especially important when they are up against them.

The Gully:

Between the slips and the point fielder is the gully fielder, who stands in the middle. They are positioned in such a way as to collect balls that may not make it to the slips due to their location.

Slip of the Leg:

A leg slip is a device that is positioned behind the batsman on the leg side. Its purpose is to catch balls that may hit the batsman on the leg.

Leg not very long:

On the leg side, the defender who plays short leg stands somewhat near to the batsman. They are positioned in such a way that they can catch balls that are deflected off of the batsman's body or bat.

Ignorant Remark:

A fielder who takes a stupid point is one who positions themselves on the leg side of the batting position relatively close to the batsman. The primary purpose of these players is to take catches and cause the batter to make errors.

The Mid-off and Mid-on Positions:

These fielders are positioned rather close to the bowler, with their bodies tilted ever-so-slightly to the off and leg sides, respectively. They are positioned in such a way as to deter the batsman from making direct hits.

Legs of a Square:

The square leg fielder stands behind the batsman on the leg side and is responsible for catching pull shots as well as balls that are flicked off the batsman's legs.

The Best Leg:

A fielder who stands behind the batter on the leg side and whose job it is to grab balls that are flicked or hooked behind the batsman is known as fine leg.

Main Idea:

The position of point is behind the batsman on the off side of the field. They are positioned there to stop diagonal cuts and deflections that head toward the off side of the field.

Lie under:

In order to stop runs from getting through the covers and make catches off cover drives, cover fielders are stationed on the off side of the field.

The positioning of fielders is a fluid component of the game, and captains constantly make adjustments to it in order to capitalize on the opposition's vulnerabilities and increase the number of opportunities for wickets. It is possible to exert pressure on the batsmen by strategic field placement, which can ultimately result in dismissals and improve the fielding side's position.

The elegance and strategic depth of cricket are in large part due to the design of the playing ground and the cricket equipment used. Every aspect of the game, from the well-known cricket bat and ball to the careful maintenance of the playing surface, plays a significant part in determining how the game unfolds. Field placement in particular is a strategic feature that is used by captains and bowlers to take advantage of the deficiencies of the opposition and generate opportunities for success.

One's understanding for the enduring allure of cricket is enhanced by developing a deeper familiarity with the intricacies of cricket equipment as well as the subtleties of field layout. Cricket's equipment and field layout are at the center of the sport's attractiveness and the enduring passion it provokes among players and fans all over the world. Whether it's the precision of a well-struck shot, the skilful movement of a bowler, or the cunning positioning of fielders, cricket's equipment and field layout are at the heart of the sport's appeal.

Chapter 2

Physical Benefits of Playing Cricket

Cricket, which is frequently lauded for the strategic depth it requires and the depth of its heritage, is a sport that is not only intellectually fascinating but also physically demanding. When cricket players hit the field, they take part in a variety of different physical exercises, all of which contribute to their overall fitness and sense of well-being. In this in-depth investigation, we look into the many different physical benefits of playing cricket. These benefits include the development of strength, endurance, agility, and cardiovascular fitness, in addition to the good impact on balance, hand-eye coordination, and body composition.

Fitness of the Cardiovascular System:

Cricket is a sport that requires short bursts of high-intensity action, including as running between the wickets, chasing the ball around the field, and making sharp adjustments in one's line of movement. This pattern of activity, which consists of periods of rest and movement, is fantastic for improving cardiovascular fitness. Players need to be able to keep up a healthy heart rate, remain calm under pressure, and recuperate rapidly in between bouts of strenuous physical activity. In limited-overs variants of the game, such as One Day Internationals (ODIs) and Twenty20 (T20) matches, where running between the wickets and quick fielding are vital, the aerobic demands of cricket become increasingly obvious. As a consequence of this, playing cricket can lead to improvements in both the player's heart health and their cardiovascular fitness.

The Power and Strength of the Muscles:

The sport of cricket entails a number of different activities, all of which call for a high level of muscular strength and power. Batsmen require upper body strength to perform powerful shots, whilst bowlers rely on lower body strength to generate speed and precision in their deliveries. Upper body strength is required for batting, while lower body strength is required for bowling. To maintain their stamina while standing in the field for extended periods of time and to throw the ball with sufficient force, fielders require strength in both their upper and lower bodies. The ability to hold a squatting stance requires wicketkeepers to have strong legs, while having power in the upper body helps wicketkeepers dive for catches. Playing cricket helps players build their muscular strength and power, which in turn contributes to improved overall physical fitness.

Rapidity of Reaction and Dexterity:

The sport of cricket is one that requires players to be agile since they need to be able to move rapidly and change direction in response to the trajectory of the ball or the actions of their opponent. Batsmen and bowlers are required to modify their swings and stances in response to the movement of the ball in order to be successful. In order to successfully catch or gather the ball, wicketkeepers need to have a lot of agility. This agility, along with quick reactions, is something that can be improved through practice and experience playing matches, and it is a key physical asset that may aid players both on and off the field.

The capacity to endure:

Cricket matches may run quite a long time, especially when they are played in the Test format, which can go on for as long as five days. The players in these matches are required to maintain their endurance throughout the entirety of the game, which may be quite taxing on the body, particularly for bowlers who may be required to bowl for extended stretches at a time. In forms with a restricted number of overs, players are required to maintain their stamina in order to meet the challenges posed by running, bowling, and fielding. Individuals can significantly improve their levels of endurance and their capacity to resist the effects of physical stress for longer periods of time if they play cricket on a regular basis.

Ability to flex and move in a range of positions:

Players in cricket are required to execute a diverse range of motions throughout the game, including sprinting, bending, stretching, and diving. The increased flexibility and range of motion that result from doing so many different types of exercises is quite beneficial. Batsmen need to have strong flexibility in order to play an effective variety of shots, whilst bowlers need it in order to keep their bowling movements correct. In order to dive, reach for catches, and avoid boundaries, fielders need to have a lot of agility and flexibility. Not only does increasing flexibility and range of motion contribute to general physical well-being, but it also helps players perform better in cricket by lowering their risk of injury and improving their overall performance.

Coordination of the Hands and Eyes:

The sport of cricket requires players to have great hand-eye coordination because they must immediately judge the line and length of the delivery and respond with precision. Batsmen have to have impeccable timing for their shots, while fielders have to be quick and accurate in their catches. Wicketkeepers are also largely reliant on their hand-eye coordination in order to gather the ball and make quick attempts at stumping and running out batters. The cultivation of this talent through participation in cricket has the potential to have a positive impact on other facets of life and can be beneficial to a variety of jobs that are performed every day that require hand-eye coordination.

Stability and Strength in the Core:

Players of cricket are required to have good balance at all times, but especially when they are hitting shots or fielding ground balls. Maintaining your equilibrium is absolutely necessary in order to execute precise movements, whether you're a batsman hitting a cover drive or a fielder diving to make a catch. In addition, having a strong core is essential for ensuring stability as well as adding force to your shoots and throws. Core strength is essential for bowlers, as it helps them keep their bodies in the right position and generate more force in their deliveries. Players have the opportunity to strengthen their core muscles and enhance their general balance by participating in frequent cricket practice.

Enhanced Improvements in Body Composition:

Cricket is a sport that can help players enhance their overall body composition. In cricket training, a mix of cardiorespiratory activity, strength training, and flexibility exercises can assist players in lowering their overall body fat percentage and increasing their percentage of lean muscle mass. Not only is it vital for maintaining a balanced body composition for cricket performance, but it is also essential for maintaining overall health and well-being. Participating in cricket on a regular basis might assist individuals in achieving and sustaining a healthy body weight as well as physique.

Management of One's Weight:

The need for physical fitness and endurance that cricket requires makes it a potentially useful activity for weight management. The fact that playing this sport burns calories, particularly when played for extended periods of time, might assist players in either maintaining a healthy weight or reducing excess body weight. Cricket may be an interesting and entertaining approach for individuals to attain their fitness objectives, which can be helpful for those persons who are seeking to reduce weight. The sport's format, which alternates between periods of intensive activity and small times of rest, makes it an excellent choice for managing one's weight and maximizing the number of calories burned.

The state of one's mind:

Playing cricket has a positive impact on one's mental health in addition to the many physical benefits it provides. Endorphins are related with the release of endorphins, which can boost mood and reduce stress when one participates in physically active pursuits such as cricket. The fact that cricket is played strategically and with a focus on teams encourages a sense of belonging and camaraderie, both of which can have a beneficial effect on mental health. After a round of cricket, players frequently report feeling a sense of contentment, relaxation, and an overall improvement in their mental well-being.

Access for All and Various Accommodations:

Cricket is one of the few sports that can accommodate players of varying ages and skill levels, which is one of the sport's defining characteristics. Cricket can be adapted to accommodate players of varying skill levels and physical capacities, which means that its players of all ages can reap the benefits of the sport's positive effects on their bodies. For instance, shorter formats such as Twenty Twenty (T20) and indoor cricket are designed for quicker gaming and may be more accessible to newbies or people with physical impairments. In addition, a large number of cricket clubs and organizations provide opportunities for younger players, female players, and players with disabilities. This fosters an inclusive environment and makes the sport more approachable to a wider audience.

Cricket is a sport that provides its participants with a wide range of health advantages, including improvements in their cardiovascular fitness, muscular strength, agility, endurance, flexibility, hand-eye coordination, balance, core strength, body composition, and weight management. In addition to these physical benefits, playing cricket can also have a significant impact on mental well-being while simultaneously fostering a sense of camaraderie and inclusiveness.

Cricket is a great option for individuals who are interested in participating in a sport that not only offers a variety of advantages for one's physical condition but also boasts a lengthy history and a high degree of strategic sophistication. The sport's perennial allure, which ranges from the thrill of a perfectly placed shot to the fulfillment of a well-executed delivery, helps to make it a cherished and loved hobby that continues to enthrall players as well as viewers.

2.1 Cardiovascular fitness and endurance

Maintaining one's entire physical health and sense of well-being requires a significant contribution from cardiovascular fitness and endurance. These two aspects of fitness are inextricably linked to one another and are necessary for sustaining a wide variety of biological processes, including as effective circulation, enhanced oxygen delivery to tissues, and the capacity to engage in extended periods of physical activity without becoming fatigued. In this extensive investigation, we dig into the relevance of cardiovascular fitness and endurance, their impact on health, as well as the numerous tactics and exercises that may be implemented to strengthen these key parts of a person's physical well-being.

Comprehending the Importance of Cardiovascular Fitness:

Cardiovascular fitness, which is also referred to as aerobic fitness, is the ability of the heart, lungs, and blood vessels to efficiently carry oxygen and nutrients to the muscles of the body during prolonged physical activity. This ability is referred to as "cardiovascular fitness." It is a measurement of the body's ability to carry out activities that need endurance and stamina for an extended period of time.

An individual who has strong cardiovascular fitness is able to participate in activities such as running, cycling, swimming, and brisk walking for lengthy periods of time without becoming overly fatigued or having excessive shortness of breath.

**The Importance of Maintaining a Healthy Cardiovascular Fitness Level:
Improved Conditions for the Heart:**

Aerobic exercise, especially when performed on a regular basis, is known to improve cardiovascular fitness and is connected with better heart health. It does this by making the heart muscle stronger, which in turn allows the heart to pump blood more effectively and efficiently throughout the body. When your heart health is better, your chance of developing cardiovascular disorders including heart attacks, strokes, and high blood pressure goes down.

Circulation that is Improved:

Fitness in the cardiovascular system encourages good blood circulation, which in turn ensures that oxygen and nutrients are efficiently transported to the body's many tissues and organs. The elimination of waste products and poisons from the body is facilitated by improved circulation, which also contributes to improved general health and vigor.

Management of One's Weight:

Participating in aerobic activities that improve cardiovascular fitness can help one maintain their weight more effectively. Participating in aerobic activity on a consistent basis helps burn calories and fat, which in turn contributes to the upkeep of a healthy body weight. This is especially helpful in lowering the likelihood of developing obesity and the health concerns that come along with it.

Enhanced Capacity for Accumulating Energy:

People who have strong cardiovascular fitness typically enjoy increased levels of energy as well as improved levels of stamina. Regular aerobic exercise improves the body's ability to make use of oxygen, which in turn leads to increased levels of energy production and a reduction in sensations of exhaustion and lethargic behavior.

Relaxation Techniques:

It is well known that cardiovascular activity can trigger the release of endorphins, which are the body's natural compounds that enhance mood. Because of this, one may experience less stress, an improvement in mental health, and a more upbeat perspective on life.

Acquiring Knowledge of Endurance:

The capacity of the body to continue engaging in strenuous exercise for an extended amount of time is known as endurance. It is a measurement of how effectively the body can sustain continuous activity and maintain performance without experiencing undue weariness or depletion. This ability is referred to as aerobic capacity. Muscular endurance is the ability of specific muscles to perform repetitive movements over time. Cardiovascular endurance is the ability of the body to perform continuous, rhythmic activities such as running, swimming, or cycling for extended periods of time. Endurance can be broken down into these two categories.

**The value of having a strong ability to endure:
Enhanced Capabilities in Athletic Competition:**

Performance in sports that call for continuous physical activity, such as long-distance running, cycling, and swimming, all need athletes to have a high level of endurance. Endurance is one of the most important factors in determining overall athletic ability. Athletes who have a high level of endurance are able to keep their top performance for extended periods of time, providing them an advantage over other competitors in their particular sports.

Enhanced Capacity in Both the Body and the Mind:

Those who have a high level of endurance tend to have improved levels of both physical and mental stamina. They are able to carry out the activities of daily living with better ease and efficiency, suffer less fatigue, and keep a higher degree of attention and focus throughout the course of the day.

Extended Capability to Work :

The body's work capacity can be increased by endurance training, which enables individuals to participate in physically demanding activities for longer periods of time without experiencing a substantial drop in their level of performance. This is especially helpful for people whose jobs need them to be physically active for long periods of time, such as those in the military, firefighters, or manual work.

Efficiency of the Metabolic System:

Training over longer periods of time improves the metabolic efficiency of the body, which in turn leads to increased energy usage and a more efficient utilization of sources of stored energy, such as carbs and fats. This may lead to improved weight management as well as metabolic health in general.

Enhanced Capacity of the Respiratory System:

Training for endurance can also improve respiratory function, leading to increased lung capacity as well as efficiency. Because of this, oxygen can be exchanged more efficiently, which enables the body to fulfill the higher oxygen needs that occur during physical exercise while also lowering the chance of developing respiratory conditions.

Techniques for Improving Cardiovascular Endurance and Fitness:

Exercises of an Aerobic Nature:

To enhance your cardiovascular fitness and endurance, it is recommended that you participate in regular aerobic activities such as running, swimming, cycling, and brisk walking. Aim to complete at least 150 minutes of aerobic activity per week at a moderate intensity or at least 75 minutes of aerobic activity per week at a high intensity.

Training with Intervals:

Your exercise program should include interval training, which consists of alternating between periods of high-intensity activity and periods of recovery exercise performed at a reduced level. This strategy has the potential to greatly improve one's cardiovascular fitness as well as their endurance.

Workouts on a Circuit:

Participate in circuit training, which entails performing a series of exercises in fast succession in order to target different groups of muscles. The endurance of both the muscles and the cardiovascular system can be improved by circuit training.

Interleaving workouts:

Participate in a wide range of different types of physical activity to prevent boredom and to work out a number of muscle groups. Alternating between two or more different types of exercise can assist increase overall fitness levels and reduce the risk of overuse problems caused by performing the same motions repeatedly.

Working Out Your Muscles:

In order to develop the strength and endurance of your muscles, you need include strength training activities in your normal workout program. Increasing your muscle strength can help improve your physical performance as a whole and contribute to higher levels of endurance.

Training That Is Consistent:

Maintain a workout regimen that is both constant and progressive to gradually enhance your cardiovascular fitness and endurance over the course of time. When it comes to accomplishing long-term fitness objectives and sustaining excellent physical health, consistency is the most important factor.

Adequate Consumption of Food and Drink:

To support your general health as well as your physical performance, eat a diet that is well balanced and abundant in nutrients, vitamins, and minerals. Maintaining proper hydration levels prior to, during, and after physical activity is essential for achieving peak performance and avoiding dehydration.

Fitness in the cardiovascular system and endurance are two essential elements that contribute to one's overall physical health and well-being. Individuals can dramatically enhance their levels of cardiovascular fitness and endurance by performing regular aerobic exercises, interval training, circuit training, cross-training, strength training, and maintaining good nutrition and hydration. Cross-training refers to performing two or more different types of resistance training on opposite sides of the body. These improvements not only result in better physical health but also contribute to improved mental well-being, increased levels of energy, and an overall improvement in the quality of life. An investment in long-term health and vitality, regular physical activity that focuses on developing cardiovascular fitness and endurance encourages a healthier and more active lifestyle overall.

2.2 Strength and agility

A person's general health and well-being are significantly impacted by their level of physical fitness, specifically their levels of both strength and agility, which are two fundamental components of physical fitness. Agility can be defined as the capacity to move rapidly and easily while maintaining precision, whereas strength refers to the ability to exert force against opposition. They work synergistically to improve overall physical performance, reduce the risk of injury, and raise the bar for one's quality of life. In this in-depth investigation, we look into the relevance of strength and agility, their impact on health, as well as the numerous workouts and tactics that may be adopted to develop these essential components of one's physical fitness.

Comprehending the Meaning of Strength:

Muscles have the potential to generate force in order to overcome barriers when they are strong. It is an essential component of physical fitness that has an effect on a variety of elements of day-to-day living, from carrying groceries and climbing stairs to taking part in sports and ensuring correct posture. Strength in the muscles can be improved by the use of certain workouts, and it is typically broken down into three primary categories:

The Unmatched Power of:

The utmost amount of force that a muscle or group of muscles can produce in a single contraction is known as their absolute strength. Powerlifting, for example, requires competitors to lift the largest possible weights for a single repetition, hence this type of strength is absolutely essential for success in this sport.

Endurance of the Muscles:

The capacity of a muscle or muscle group to apply force repeatedly or to maintain a contraction

for an extended length of time is what we mean when we talk about muscular endurance. It is of utmost significance in sports and activities such as running, swimming, and cycling because these need continuous activation of the muscles.

Strength for Explosions:

The capacity to generate force in a short amount of time is the defining characteristic of explosive strength, which is sometimes referred to as power. This type of strength is necessary in activities like as sprinting and jumping, which require the athlete to rapidly contract their muscles in order to achieve their best possible performance.

The Significance of Having a Strong Body:

Improved Capacity for Physical Activity:

Strength training helps improve a person's physical performance in a variety of settings, including athletics, weightlifting, and daily activities. It enables athletes to lift higher weights, do daily activities and competitive sports with greater comfort, and improve their overall performance overall.

Prevention of Bodily Harm:

By helping to stabilize joints and improving muscular balance, strength training can reduce the risk of injuries caused by muscle imbalances or bad posture. The support and protection that strong muscles provide against strains, sprains, and other ailments is invaluable.

Advantages to One's Metabolism:

Because the metabolic rate of muscle tissue is higher than that of fat tissue, people who have a greater proportion of muscle in their bodies burn more calories even when they are at rest. Both the control of one's weight and the general health of one's metabolism can benefit from this.

Improved Conditions of the Bone:

Strength training causes the bones to undergo stress, which increases bone density and decreases the likelihood of developing osteoporosis and fractures. It is of particular value to people as they progress into their later years.

Enhancements to the Functionality:

For daily functional activities like bending, lifting, reaching, and standing, having muscles that are strong is absolutely necessary. People who have adequate muscular strength are able to keep their independence and continue to participate in these activities with less difficulty as they get older.

Acquiring an Understanding of Agility:

The ability to move rapidly and smoothly while keeping one's balance, coordination, and precision intact is what we mean when we talk about agility. It requires a variety of different physical abilities, including as quickness, balance, flexibility, and response time, among others. Agility is an essential component of physical fitness and is of great benefit in a wide variety of sports and activities that call for quick and active movements.

The Crucial Role of Adaptability:

The Performance in Sports:

Sports like soccer, basketball, and tennis all require a high level of agility from their competitors because these games include frequent directional shifts. Athletes that have a high level of agility are able to move around the playing field or court with ease, giving them a competitive advantage and increasing their overall effectiveness.

Prevention of Bodily Harm:

Strength exercise helps improve joint stability, coordination, and body control, and agility training is a great way to get started. Increased agility can make a person less likely to sustain injuries, particularly those that are the result of falls or unexpected movements.

Maintaining both Balance and Coordination:

Exercises that focus on agility help enhance one's balance and coordination, both of which are vital for preserving correct posture and warding off falls. Improved balance is associated with greater improvements in one's general state of physical health.

Movement That Is Functional:

The ability to move quickly and deftly through congested areas, avoid obstacles, and respond effectively to unforeseen circumstances are all important aspects of agility that are useful in everyday life. It strengthens a person's capability to react appropriately in changing environments.

Advantages to One's Mind:

A lot of the time, mental obstacles are included in agility training because individuals are required to react swiftly to different stimuli. This has the potential to improve cognitive abilities including recall and concentration, as well as decision-making.

Techniques to Improve Both Your Strength and Your Agility:

Working Out Your Muscles:

Strengthen your muscles by performing exercises that use your own bodyweight, free weights, resistance bands, or weight machines. Squats, deadlifts, bench presses, and rows should all be included in a comprehensive strength training program in order to target diverse muscle groups and ensure that the program is well-rounded. The key to consistently testing the muscles and boosting strength growth is to perform workouts that involve progressive overload.

Jumping Exercises: Plyometrics

Plyometric exercises, such as squat jumps, box jumps, and burpees, should be incorporated into your workout routine if you want to improve your explosive strength and agility. These workouts strengthen the body's capacity to create force in a short amount of time and involve fast muscular contractions.

Movements That Serve a Function:

Put your attention on movements that are functional and that imitate things you do in real life. These movements work a wide variety of muscle groups, which not only improves muscular coordination but also increases agility. Lunges, step-ups, and medicine ball throws are some examples of such exercises.

Exercises to Improve Your Balance and Coordination:

Include activities that challenge your balance and coordination in the workout plan you follow. Exercises like standing on one leg and using balance boards or stability balls can assist improve both balance and coordination. These exercises are very beneficial for reducing the risk of accidents and improving general functionality in daily life.

Exercises to Improve Your Speed and Agility:

Take part in speed and agility workouts that entail making sudden changes of direction, such as shuttle runs, ladder drills, and cone drills. This type of practice is especially useful for improving athletic performance.

Interleaving workouts:

In order to avoid being bored with your workouts and to test new areas of your strength and agility, try mixing up the kind of activities that you often do. Activities such as swimming, yoga, and martial arts can all be considered forms of cross-training.

The importance of flexibility and stretching:

Include stretching exercises in your routine to increase your flexibility. Flexibility is a key component in complementing both strength and agility. Protecting yourself from injury and enhancing your range of motion both depend on your ability to keep a healthy level of flexibility.

Appropriate Recuperation and Nutrition:

It is important to eat a well-balanced diet that is high in nutrients in order to assist the growth and repair of muscle. After periods of strength and agility training, it is important to drink enough water and put an emphasis on rest and recovery in order to provide muscles the opportunity to mend and expand.

Both strength and agility are key components of physical fitness that have a substantial influence on an individual's overall quality of life as well as their health and physical performance. Strength training is beneficial for improving physical strength, preventing injuries, and enhancing metabolic health. Agility training, on the other hand, is beneficial for improving a person's speed, balance, coordination, and cognitive skills. Individuals can improve their strength and agility by combining workouts and techniques that target these characteristics of physical fitness, which ultimately leads to improved overall health and a higher degree of physical well-being. The dynamic combo of strength and agility plays a crucial role in boosting an individual's physical capabilities and fostering a healthier and more active lifestyle. This is true whether the goal is to improve athletic performance, reduce the risk of injury, or improve day-to-day functionality.

2.3 Hand-eye coordination and reflexes

Hand-eye coordination and reflexes are two interrelated talents that play a key role in a wide variety of physical activities and daily chores. Reflexes are especially important in situations where there is a rapid change in direction. Hand-eye coordination is the seamless collaboration between the visual system and the motor system that enables accurate control and manipulation of objects depending on what the eyes perceive. Hand-eye coordination is often referred to as "two-hand coordination" or "two-limb coordination." On the other hand, reflexes are quick reactions that are automatic and involve both the sensory and motor pathways of the nervous system. They are triggered by external stimuli. In this in-depth investigation, we look into the relevance of hand-eye coordination and reflexes, their impact on physical performance, as well as the numerous exercises and tactics that may be implemented to increase these essential facets of one's physical fitness. These topics are covered since hand-eye coordination and reflexes are two of the most important parts of one's physical fitness.

Comprehending the Relationship Between the Hands and the Eyes:

The capacity to coordinate visual input with motor skills is referred to as hand-eye coordination. This enables a person to make actions that are precise and accurate. It entails the effective processing of visual information, such as the path and position of an item, which is then followed by the execution of a motor reaction, such as catching a ball, striking a target, or threading a needle. For example. Coordination of the hands and eyes is essential for a wide variety of activities, including sports, the playing of musical instruments, surgical procedures, and even seemingly insignificant occupations such as writing and typing.

The Importance of Coordinating Your Eyes and Hands:
The Performance in Sports:

Hand-eye coordination is especially important in sports like cricket, baseball, tennis, and archery, which require the athlete to aim, catch, or strike an object. Other examples include the word. Athletes who have exceptional hand-eye coordination have a competitive advantage because it enables them to hit targets more consistently, make accurate throws, and catch balls that are moving quickly.

Typical Activities:

Hand-eye coordination is required for many activities that are common in everyday life, such as driving, cooking, sewing, and using tools. It grants individuals the ability to carry out these actions with precision and accuracy, which contributes to increased productivity and safety.

Skills in both the Fine and Gross Motor Systems:

Hand-eye coordination includes both fine motor abilities and gross motor skills. Some examples

of fine motor skills include being able to thread a needle or play an instrument, while examples of huge motor skills include being able to catch a ball or ride a bicycle. The development of these abilities improves a person's overall physical performance as well as their functionality.

The development of one's mind includes:

Developing better hand-eye coordination can help one's cognitive abilities, including their ability to pay attention, concentrate, and be aware of their spatial surroundings. The capacity of the brain to receive visual information and transfer that processing into regulated motor responses is enhanced as a result of this.

Recognizing and Explaining Reflexes:

Reflexes that are innate:

Reflexes that are inborn are automatic responses that are either present at birth or develop shortly after birth. Inborn reflexes are sometimes referred to as primitive reflexes. The Moro reaction, often known as the startle response, is one example. Another is the sucking reflex. Reflexes that are innate to an individual are necessary for both survival and the early development of motor abilities.

Reflexes That Have Been Acquired or Conditioned:

Acquired reflexes are responses that are learnt via experience and practice, and they grow with time. Ivan Pavlov's research with dogs in classical conditioning provide a good illustration of the conditioned reflex, which occurs when a stimulus that is at first unrelated to a response comes to be connected with that reaction after it has been paired with it multiple times.

The Crucial Role That Reflexes Play:

Mechanisms for Self-Defense:

The initiation of quick responses to stimuli that could be detrimental is the function of reflexes, which serve as protective mechanisms. For example, the withdrawal reflex causes the quick withdrawal of a limb from a painful stimulation in order to protect it from being injured in any way.

Change: adaptation

Individuals are able to adapt to changing circumstances thanks to reflexes, which enable them to respond rapidly to shifting sensory information. During movement, for instance, the stretch reflex is responsible for maintaining the length and tone of the muscles.

Functionalities of the Mind:

The capacity of the brain to interpret sensory information and to launch the most suitable motor responses can be shaped by reflexes, which can also have an effect on cognitive abilities. This relationship between reflexes and cognitive development can have significant repercussions for learning and the ability to solve problems in a variety of contexts.

Techniques that Can Help You Improve Your Hand-Eye Coordination and Reflexes:

Training for the Eye's Tracking Ability:

Exercises in visual tracking need you to follow the movement of things with your eyes, thus you should engage in these types of activities. Juggling, following the path of a ball, or following patterns with your sight are all examples of activities that fall within this category.

Ball sports include:

Play ball games like tennis, table tennis, or racquetball, which demand you to keep track of an object that is moving quickly and respond with accurate hand movements. These activities are fantastic for enhancing your hand-eye coordination as well as your reflexes.

Exercises in Reaction:

Reaction activities like the "Simon Says" game, which needs a quick response to spoken directions, should be practiced. The cognitive and motor functions are both improved through the use of these exercises, which also helps to develop the relationship between perception and action.

Shooting at a Target:

Participate in target shooting activities such as archery or shooting, where accurate aiming and shooting skills are required, and have fun doing so. These pursuits require an extremely high level of hand-eye coordination as well as finely trained reflexes.

Participating in Musical Performances by Playing:

Hand-eye coordination and fine motor abilities can be considerably improved by learning to play a musical instrument, particularly one such as the piano or violin that requires intricate finger motions.

Testing Your Reflexes:

In order to evaluate your reflexes, a trained medical expert may do something called a reflex test. This can be helpful in identifying any problems or irregularities and guiding actions, should they be required.

A sense of equilibrium and proprioception:

Reflexes can be indirectly improved with the help of exercises that promote stability and efficient movement. These exercises focus on improving balance and proprioception, which is the awareness of where the body is in space. In this sense, the practice of yoga and other forms of balance training can be helpful.

Games That Train Your Brain:

Hand-eye coordination and reflexes can be improved by playing brain-training games or using apps on a mobile device that present a challenge to cognitive skills and visual-motor integration.

Coordination of the hands and eyes, as well as reflexes, are essential components of physical fitness that play a role in an individual's capacity to carry out activities that are exact and correct as well as to react quickly to stimuli. Individuals can improve their hand-eye coordination and reflexes through the use of specific workouts and tactics that target these abilities. This can lead to improved physical performance and functionality in a variety of activities, including sports, daily tasks, and cognitive processes. The strength of accuracy in hand-eye coordination and reflexes plays a crucial part in defining an individual's physical capabilities and fostering a healthier and more agile lifestyle. This is true whether it is for competitive sports, the development of fine motor skills, or cognitive development.

2.4 Weight management and calorie burn

The ability to maintain a healthy weight and the amount of calories burned each day are two interrelated aspects that have a substantial influence on an individual's overall physical health and well-being. A healthy weight can be achieved and maintained by striking a balance between the amount of calories that are taken and the number of calories that are expended throughout the course of a day through a variety of activities and metabolic processes.

In this in-depth investigation, we delve into the relevance of weight management and calorie burn, their impact on health, and the numerous strategies and tactics that can be used to reach and maintain a healthy weight while encouraging overall well-being. In addition, we discuss the various strategies and techniques that may be followed to achieve and maintain a healthy weight.

Comprehending the Art of Weight Management:

The practice of reaching and maintaining a healthy body weight within a certain range that is deemed optimal for an individual's age, height, and gender is referred to as weight management. Weight management refers to the process of achieving and maintaining a healthy body weight. It entails making deliberate decisions about one's diet, level of physical activity, and overall lifestyle in order to avoid excessive weight gain, encourage fat loss, and keep the body's composition in a balanced state.

The Importance of Maintaining a Healthy Weight:
Wellness and the Avoidance of Illness:

Keeping a healthy weight is an important step in the prevention of a number of different health concerns, including cardiovascular disease, diabetes, high blood pressure, and even some forms of cancer. The excessive gain of weight, also known as obesity, is a risk factor for various disorders and can have a negative impact on an individual's overall health.

Functionality of the Physical Body:

Getting to a healthy weight and keeping it off are both important factors in improving one's physical functionality and mobility. It eases the pressure that is placed on joints, which in turn lowers the chance of developing problems that are associated with the joints and makes it possible to do daily activities with greater efficiency.

Wellness from a Psychological Perspective:

A person's ability to maintain a healthy weight can have a beneficial effect on both their self-esteem and their perception of their bodies. Getting to a healthy weight typically results in an increase in one's sense of self-confidence and a more upbeat perspective on life.

Increased Satisfaction with Life:

There is a correlation between having a healthy weight and having a greater quality of life. People who keep their weight within a healthy range have a stronger sense of well-being, higher energy levels, and fewer health-related limits than those whose weight falls outside of the healthy range.

Comprehending the Role of Calorie Burn:

The quantity of calories that are used up by the body in the course of its various physiological processes and activities is referred to as the "calorie burn." Calorie burn is also known as calorie expenditure or energy expenditure. Calories are burned off continuously by the body in order to support essential tasks such as breathing, regulating body temperature, and facilitating fundamental metabolic processes. In addition, the amount of calories burned throughout the day is affected by things like daily activities, exercise, and chores.

The significance of calorie expenditure is as follows:

Management of One's Weight:

The rate at which calories are burned is an essential component of weight management. A person needs to produce a calorie deficit in order to lose weight. This occurs when the number of calories burned is greater than the number of calories taken during the course of the day. On the other hand, in order to keep the same weight, it is necessary to strike a balance between the calories you consume and the calories you expend.

The state of one's metabolism:

Burning calories has an impact on the efficiency of energy usage and the distribution of nutrients, which in turn has an effect on metabolic health. The function of the metabolism can be improved through regular physical activity and exercise, which can result in improved glucose regulation and utilization of fat.

Heart and Blood Vessel Health:

The improvement of heart and lung function, reduction in the risk of cardiovascular disease, and promotion of healthy blood pressure and cholesterol levels are some of the ways that engaging in physical activities that boost calorie burn can improve cardiovascular health.

The endurance and strength of the muscles:

Increasing the number of calories burned by exercising and participating in other physical activities that also promotes muscle strength and endurance. Because muscle tissue burns more calories at rest than fat tissue does, the contribution that muscle tissue makes to calorie expenditure is significant.

Affect and General Health:

The release of endorphins can be stimulated by engaging in activities that increase calorie burn. This can contribute to an improvement in mood, a reduction in stress, and an overall improvement in well-being.

Techniques for Efficient Control of One's Weight and the Burning of Calories:
Diet That Is Balanced:

Adopt a diet that is both balanced and nutritious, providing all of the essential elements while keeping the calorie consumption under control. Put most of your attention on foods that are whole, such as fruits, vegetables, lean proteins, and grains that are whole. It is important to limit your intake of meals that are heavy in calories, sugar, and processed ingredients.

Keeping Tabs on Your Calories

Use meal diaries or mobile applications to keep track of the number of calories you consume. This technique can assist in increasing awareness of eating routines and make it simpler to maintain control over the amount of calories consumed.

Controlling Portions:

To prevent yourself from overeating, make it a habit to regulate your portions. Consuming fewer calories overall by eating meals that are more moderately sized can help people lose weight.

Maintaining a Regular Exercise Routine:

To accelerate the rate at which calories are burned, you should engage in frequent physical activity and exercise. Include activities that will get your heart rate up, exercises that will build muscle, and stretching into your program.

High-Intensity Interval Training, or HIIT for short:

Include bouts of high-intensity interval training in your regular regimen of working out. High-intensity interval training (HIIT) consists of shorter bouts of more strenuous exercise followed by more moderate recovery periods. This strategy has the potential to burn more calories and improve one's cardiovascular fitness.

Strength Training Using Resistance:

In order to gain muscle mass, your workouts should include resistance training activities. Because muscle tissue has a greater metabolic rate than fat tissue, people who have more muscle tend to burn more calories even when they are at rest.

Typical Activities:

Put forth the effort to remain active all through the day by finding ways to include physical activity into your day-to-day activities.

Taking the stairs instead of the elevator, walking or riding a bike instead of driving, and standing instead of sitting are all simple things that can help burn calories.

Raise your level of NEAT:

The term "Non-Exercise Activity Thermogenesis" (NEAT) refers to the calories burned during daily activities that do not involve physical exercise. These activities include walking, standing, and fidgeting. An increase in NEAT can have a considerable impact on a person's total caloric expenditure.

The role of Sleep in Recovery:

Make getting enough rest and recovering a top priority. Insufficiency in sleep can cause hormonal imbalance, which in turn can lead to an increase in calorie consumption and a subsequent gain in weight.

Keep yourself hydrated:

Maintaining a healthy level of hydration is beneficial to the body as a whole and can assist in appetite regulation. It's not uncommon for people to confuse thirst with hunger, which might result in eating more calories than necessary.

The maintenance of a healthy weight and the burning of calories are essential elements of an active and healthy lifestyle. A well-balanced strategy to calorie consumption and expenditure, with a primary emphasis on nutrient-dense diet and consistent physical activity, is necessary for achieving and sustaining a healthy weight. Effective control of one's weight not only improves one's general health but also makes a positive contribution to one's well-being and the overall quality of one's life. Individuals can get on the path to living a life that is healthier, more energized, and more rewarding by adopting techniques that are congruent with leading an active lifestyle and eating in a way that is healthy.

2.5 Injury prevention and safety measures

Injury prevention and safety precautions are vital components of ensuring that persons can participate in a variety of activities, sports, and daily duties without the chance of getting injured. These components are also essential for preserving one's physical well-being. Adopting safety precautions and keeping injury prevention in mind while engaging in sporting and recreational activities, whether at home or in the workplace, can considerably cut down on the probability of experiencing an accident or injury in any of these settings. We go into the significance of injury prevention, the influence of safety measures, and numerous tactics for safeguarding physical well-being as we continue this conversation.

The Importance of Attempting to Avoid Injuries:
Upholding the Existing Standard of Living:

The prevention of injuries is an essential component in the upkeep of an individual's quality of life. Injuries can result in discomfort, pain, and limited mobility, all of which can make it difficult for a person to carry out the activities of daily living and participate in the pursuits that bring them pleasure.

Bringing Down the Costs of Healthcare:

Injuries almost always result in additional medical costs, which may include hospitalization, rehabilitation, and therapy that continues over time. The financial burden that is placed on individuals and healthcare systems is reduced when injuries are avoided.

Fostering Health Over the Long Term:

Accidents can cause injuries that have long-term effects on one's health, such as the development of chronic illnesses or impairments. Taking precautions to avoid getting hurt is really necessary in order to avoid these chronic health problems.

Increasing Workforce Productivity:

Injuries sustained on the job might result in lost work time and lower over-all productivity. Injury prevention in the workplace is beneficial to both employers and employees because it helps to maintain an environment that is both safe and productive.

The Effects of Precautionary Measures:

Where You Are:

Accidents and injuries can be avoided by putting safety precautions into place within the home. This involves taking precautions such as placing handrails on steps, fastening carpets to prevent slipping, childproofing, and ensuring that paths have adequate lighting to lessen the risk of falling over.

In the Working Environment:

Work-related accidents are avoidable if appropriate safety precautions are taken in the workplace. These precautions include providing employees with the appropriate training, personal protection equipment, and ergonomic workspaces. In addition, keeping one's workplace clean and well-organized lowers one's likelihood of being injured in an accident.

When it comes to Athletics and Recreation:

In order to avoid getting hurt while participating in sports or other leisure activities, it is important to wear the necessary protective gear and adhere to all of the rules and guidelines. It is vital to use protective equipment such as helmets, pads, and other protective gear in order to limit the risk of head injuries, fractures, and strains.

While Traveling:

It is essential to take safety precautions while driving, such as fastening seatbelts, obeying traffic regulations, and staying alert at all times in order to reduce the risk of being involved in an auto accident or suffering injuries linked to driving.

Strategies for the Prevention of Injuries:

Education and Professional Development:

It is critical to the process of injury prevention to provide education and training on various preventative safety measures as well as best practices. This includes instructing people on the proper way to move large objects, displaying the correct way to exercise, and providing safety training for various hobbies.

Equipment that is Appropriate:

It is of the utmost importance to ensure that suitable safety equipment is utilized in order to reduce the risk of injury. This refers to the use of protective gear in sports, such as helmets, padding, and footwear. At workplaces, individuals should be given with personal protection equipment and instructed on how to properly use it.

Procedures for Ensured Safety:

It is necessary to establish safety protocols both in the workplace and while participating in activities. This may include explicit guidelines for the handling of dangerous materials, safety checklists, and preparations for responding to emergency situations.

Maintenance on a Constant Basis:

Accidents can be avoided almost entirely by doing routine maintenance on all of one's assets, including equipment, cars, and buildings. The danger of accidents can be reduced by checking that all of the machinery is in good operating order, that the brakes on the cars are working properly, and that the structures are structurally sound.

The monitoring of:

In order to ensure that safety standards and guidelines are adhered to, it is essential to have adequate supervision present throughout sporting events and leisure activities, particularly when children are involved. The ability of supervisors to watch people and identify potential hazards is another reason why supervision is so important in the workplace.

Analyzing the Dangers:

Individuals are able to recognize potential dangers and take preventative steps when they conduct risk assessments in their homes, in their places of employment, and while participating in sporting activities. This includes assessing the surroundings for potential hazards such as electrical hazards, the chance of slipping and falling, and more.

Sanitation and Personal Hygiene:

Accidents that are caused by mold development, vermin, and slippery flooring can be avoided by maintaining a high level of cleanliness and sanitation in living spaces as well as places of employment. In addition, practicing good hygiene helps cut down on the likelihood of getting sick or hurt due to contamination.

Ergonomics entails:

Taking into account ergonomics in the workplace is one way to reduce the risk of musculoskeletal injuries. The goal of ergonomic design is to produce working environments that reduce physical stress and discomfort to the greatest extent possible.

Consciousness of Risk:

The most important step in the process of preventing injuries is raising knowledge about safety. This includes informing people about the typical dangers that they face and the significance of taking appropriate precautions. Workshops, public awareness campaigns, and safety signs are all potential ways to increase one's level of safety awareness.

Providing First Aid and Responding to Emergencies:

It is absolutely necessary to have training in first aid and emergency response in order to respond quickly to situations involving injuries and accidents. Learning how to provide first aid to someone who has been injured can considerably lessen the severity of the condition.

It is essential to take precautions against potential dangers and injuries if one is interested in protecting their bodily and mental health. Individuals are able to lessen the likelihood of experiencing accidental injuries and illnesses in a variety of contexts, including at home, in the job, and when participating in sporting and recreational activities.

Individuals can experience an improved quality of life, decreased costs for healthcare, and enhanced productivity if they adhere to safety rules, use suitable equipment, and keep a clean and organized environment. The prevention of injuries is a shared responsibility, and the promotion of safety awareness as well as appropriate education is the key to reducing the number of accidents and the associated effects of such incidents.

Chapter 3

Mental Benefits of Cricket

In cricket, sometimes known as the "gentleman's game," it is not enough to simply be able to master the abilities of hitting, bowling, and fielding; the sport also provides a variety of mental benefits that contribute to personal development and well-being. This article examines the many ways in which the sport of cricket improves mental health, encourages resilience, helps sharpen focus, and provides a feeling of community.

Relaxation and Alleviation of Stress:

Whether you want to play or just watch, getting involved in a game of cricket can be an effective way to relieve tension. Endorphins, which are natural mood boosters, are released when a person participates in physical activity, whether that activity takes the form of playing a sport or merely cheering on a favorite team. The level of concentration that is necessary to watch a match might momentarily divert one's attention away from day-to-day stresses and help lessen levels of stress.

Enhanced Capacity for Concentration and Focus:

Players in cricket need to be able to maintain a high degree of concentration and focus at all times. The batters have to keep watch of the movement of the ball, the bowlers have to aim for specific locations, and the fielders have to be attentive for any opportunities. This intense focus on the game can increase one's cognitive capacities as well as their ability to concentrate and pay attention to detail.

Cooperation with Others and Engaging in Social Activity:

The team sport of cricket promotes social contact as well as bonding among its participants. Participating on a cricket team can help cultivate a sense of belonging and improve teamwork. Teamwork and interpersonal skills can be improved by co-operating toward the accomplishment of a common objective, such as the triumphant conclusion of a match or the smooth running of a successful partnership.

Resilience of the Mind:

Cricket, just like life, is full of both highs and lows. Players are frequently confronted with adversity, which can take the shape of difficult conditions, formidable opponents, or personal issues with performance.

Conquering these obstacles fosters mental toughness and teaches players how to maintain their composure and concentration even when the odds are stacked against them. This toughness isn't limited to just the playing field; it can be brought into everyday life and employed there.

Defining Objectives and Achieving Success:

The process of goal-setting and -accomplishment is fundamental to the sport of cricket. Players are always working toward specific goals within the context of the game, whether it is reaching a certain number of runs on the scoreboard or taking a certain number of wickets with their bowling. This strategy, which is aimed on achieving goals, can be adapted to day-to-day living, thereby assisting individuals in establishing and achieving both personal and professional goals.

Both persistence and patience are required:

Patient play is frequently called for in the sport of cricket. It's not uncommon for batsmen to spend hours at the crease, patiently waiting for the perfect opportunity to score, while bowlers remain focused on taking wickets. These characteristics of patience and persistence are valuable in many parts of life, such as making progress in one's work and developing oneself as a person.

Formulation of Strategies and Choices:

Cricket requires players to make a variety of strategic choices, ranging from where to position their fields to which shots to take. Players are required to appraise the situation, plan for their opponent's moves, and make decisions as quickly as possible. The development of skills in decision-making and strategic thinking can be useful in a variety of contexts, including professional and personal life.

Increasing One's Self-Assurance:

Gaining victories on the cricket pitch might help boost one's self-confidence. A player's self-esteem can be improved in a variety of ways, including through the scoring of runs, the taking of wickets, and outstanding fielding performances. This heightened sense of self-confidence can extend to other aspects of life, enabling individuals to take on new challenges with the self-assurance to do so successfully.

The Management of Stress:

Individuals can learn how to cope with pressure and stress by playing cricket. The mental toughness that may be developed via playing cricket provides individuals with the tools necessary to manage stress effectively and remain resilient in the face of adversity, be it during a tense moment during a match or during a trying time in their own lives.

Resilience in Emotional Aspects:

Cricket, like any other sport, features both triumph and defeat at various points throughout the game. Players need to develop the ability to respond with dignity and poise in both winning and losing situations. Having this kind of emotional resilience is extremely helpful in preserving mental health and managing the emotional ups and downs that are inevitable in life.

The Resolution of Conflict:

In cricket, as in any other team sport, there is the potential for players to argue with one another. Learning how to settle disagreements in a civilized manner is an essential part of working in a group. These skills in conflict resolution can be applied to both personal and professional relationships, contributing to improved communication and comprehension in both settings.

Management of One's Time:

The sport of cricket involves a significant time and effort investment. A key quality is the ability to efficiently manage one's time in order to maintain a healthy balance between training, matches, and one's personal life. The capacity to effectively manage one's time can assist individuals in striking a healthy balance between their personal lives, their job lives, and their family lives.

The ability to think strategically and solve problems:

The game of cricket requires players to think strategically and solve problems on multiple levels. While players are required to adjust to the ever-changing game conditions, captains devise strategies to outmaneuver the competition. These abilities translate into situations that occur in real life, empowering individuals to respond to obstacles with creative and original solutions.

Discipline de soi-même:

In the sport of cricket, having discipline is an absolutely necessary quality. They are required to stick to their training schedules, keep up with their fitness, and diligently work on improving their talents. This discipline is applicable to both one's personal and professional life, which enables individuals to maintain their concentration on their objectives.

The Connection Between Mindfulness and Mental Health:

Due to the fact that it demands players to be totally in the here and now, cricket can be considered a sort of mindfulness. This practice of mindfulness, which is developed throughout the course of play, has the potential to result in enhanced mental health. Maintaining a presence in the here and now and concentrating on the task at hand might make one feel less anxious and more at peace.

The pursuit of Pleasure and Recreation:

The game of cricket provides an outlet for fun and pleasure, allowing players to take their minds off the stresses of everyday life. Either participating in or simply watching a game that one enjoys can help to promote feelings of physical and mental well-being and relaxation.

Learning That Never Stops:

Cricket is a sport in which participants are expected to consistently improve their skills and acquire new knowledge. A culture that promotes lifelong learning can inspire individuals to accept new challenges and look for opportunities for personal development over the course of their lives.

Support and a Sense of Belonging:

Whether at the club, school, or professional level, being a part of the cricket community provides access to a network of support as well as friendship. These social relationships can contribute to mental well-being by offering a sense of belonging and a support system in times of need when the individual is in need.

3.1 Stress reduction and mental relaxation

Many people find themselves constantly burdened by stress as a result of the fast-paced and demanding environment we live in today. Our mental and physical health might suffer when we are subjected to the stresses of our jobs, families, and other personal commitments. Techniques for lowering stress and mentally relaxing oneself are absolutely necessary in order to successfully traverse this intricate environment. During this in-depth investigation, we will discuss the relevance of stress reduction, the impact of mental relaxation, and the many different ways that can assist us in locating inner peace and well-being.

Recognizing the Signs of Stress:

Experiencing stress is a normal part of a person's body's reaction to trying or potentially dangerous circumstances. This is the process by which the body gets itself ready for action. Stress can be useful if it is experienced in moderation since it can motivate us to perform well and adapt effectively to change. On the other hand, prolonged or severe stress can result in a wide variety of negative effects on both one's physical and mental health.

The Importance of Finding Ways to Reduce Stress:

The presence of chronic stress has been connected to a variety of physical health problems, such as heart disease, high blood pressure, obesity, and a compromised immune system. Stress reduction is absolutely necessary for the upkeep of general wellness.

Stress can have a negative impact on mental health, increasing the risk of conditions such as anxiety, depression, and mood disorders. Stress reduction can help ease the symptoms of various disorders and promote emotional well-being.

Enhancement of Cognitive Function High levels of stress can have a negative impact on cognitive function, including memory, concentration, and the ability to make decisions. Cognitive talents can be improved by the use of approaches that reduce stress.

Improved Relationships: Long-term stress can put a strain on personal relationships, which can lead to disagreements and misunderstandings. Reducing stress can assist in improving one's ability to communicate and connect with people.

Increased Productivity Productivity and creativity are both negatively impacted by stress. A decrease in stress levels can lead to an increase in productivity at work and in day-to-day activities.

Recognizing the Benefits of Mental Relaxation:

To relax one's mind, one must first quiet one's thoughts and then let go of any built-up mental stress. It is about achieving a condition of inner calm, when the mind is free from ideas that are racing and worrying to an excessive degree. Techniques of mental relaxation might assist persons in regaining their equilibrium and concentration.

The Importance of Releasing Tension in the Mind:

Relaxing one's mind is one of the most powerful tools available for combating the negative effects of stress. Anxiety can be alleviated, blood pressure can be lowered, and fewer negative consequences of stress can be seen on the body when individuals practice techniques that quiet the mind.

Techniques of mental relaxation such as mindfulness and meditation have been shown to increase one's ability to regulate their emotions and foster a more optimistic attitude on life. This contributes to an overall improvement in emotional well-being.

Better Sleep Better sleep can be achieved by individuals through the process of mental relaxation, which helps to quiet the mind and reduces the symptoms of insomnia and other sleep disturbances.

Strengthening one's mental resilience through the regular use of mental relaxation techniques might help individuals become better able to deal with the difficulties and setbacks that are inevitable in life.

Improved Capacity to Solve Problems: A mind that is at ease is one that is more able to solve problems and come to logical conclusions. Clear thinking can be fostered through mental relaxation.

Techniques for Reducing Mental Stress and Relaxing the Mind:

Meditation with Attention to the Present:

Meditation on mindfulness entails giving undivided attention to the happenings of the here and now without passing judgment on them. It assists people in becoming more conscious of their own thoughts and feelings, which ultimately results in a greater mental relaxation and a reduction in stress for the individual.

Exercises for Taking Deep Breaths:

Relaxation can be achieved by the practice of deep breathing techniques, such as diaphragmatic breathing. These activities help to reduce the heart rate and calm the nervous system. A significant impact on one's ability to manage stress can be achieved by devoting a brief period of time each day to the practice of deep breathing.

Relaxation of the Muscles in a Progressive Manner:

In order to alleviate tension in both the body and the mind, progressive muscle relaxation includes tensing and then relaxing distinct sets of muscles. People that carry stress in their bodies benefit tremendously from utilizing this approach because of its ability to alleviate that stress.

Yoga:

Yoga is a practice that involves holding various postures, focusing on one's breath, and meditating in order to alleviate tension, enhance flexibility, and foster mental tranquility. Practicing yoga on a regular basis might result in an increased sense of serenity and balance.

Activities in Nature and the Great Outdoors:

Spending time in natural settings and participating in activities that take place outside can have a sedative and reassuring impact on the psyche.

Mental relaxation can be achieved by the pursuit of activities such as going on a hike, gardening, or even just taking a stroll through a park.

The Expression of Creativity Through Art:

The act of participating in creative pursuits such as painting, writing, or playing a musical instrument can be a healthy outlet for expressing one's feelings as well as a source of relaxation. An escape from the strains of everyday life might be found in engaging in creative activities.

Imagery and visualization, sometimes known as Guided:

The process of producing a mental image or scenario with the purpose of inducing a state of calm and relaxation is known as guided imagery. It is an effective method for lowering levels of tension and increasing levels of mental calm.

Aromatherapy:

Aromatherapy is a technique that helps people relax by utilizing the fragrances of essential oils. Lavender and chamomile are two aromas that are known to have a relaxing effect, making them useful tools in the fight against stress.

Putting a Time Cap on Screen Use:

An excessive amount of time spent in front of a screen, particularly in the hours leading up to bedtime, can cause sleep patterns to become disrupted and contribute to stress. Less time spent in front of a screen, particularly in the evening, has been shown to improve mental relaxation and sleep quality.

Assistance from Others:

Individuals can improve their ability to deal with stress by maintaining healthy social connections and actively seeking support from friends and family. It might be emotionally beneficial to discuss the sources of stress with those you care about.

Management of One's Time:

Stress can be reduced when individuals learn to prioritize their responsibilities and avoid becoming overwhelmed through the application of effective time management. Maintaining a healthy equilibrium between one's professional and personal life is essential for mental calm.

Help from Qualified Individuals:

It is imperative that one seeks the assistance of a therapist or counselor as soon as possible in the event that stress becomes unbearable or contributes to difficulties of mental health such as anxiety or depression. Counseling and therapy can give helpful tools and support for individuals who are looking to reduce their levels of stress.

3.2 Teamwork and social bonding

Effective collaboration and social bonding play a crucial role in many aspects of life, from competitive sports to the workplace, including the accomplishment of shared objectives, the development of unity, and the promotion of a sense of belonging. Collaboration and strong social relationships have undeniably powerful effects, regardless of whether they are being utilized on a sports field, in a corporate context, or within a community. We dive into the relevance of collaboration, the impact of social bonding, and the numerous tactics and practices that contribute to the formation of strong, cohesive teams and communities as part of this in-depth investigation.

Comprehending the Importance of Teamwork:

Transfer of Information:

Communication that is both open and effective is essential for the exchange of ideas, the expression of concerns, and the resolution of conflicts. Communication that is open and honest helps to cultivate a culture of trust within a team and ensures that everyone is working toward the same goals.

Cooperative effort:

Successful teams work together to combine the varied skills, expertise, and experiences of their members in order to accomplish their shared objectives. Collaboration fosters creativity and invention, which in turn enables teams to come up with one-of-a-kind solutions to difficult situations.

Assistance to One Another:

It is vital, in order to cultivate a culture of growth and development, to have a supportive team atmosphere in which members of the team assist each other, offer advice to one another, and provide constructive feedback to one another. When members of a team help each other out, it fosters a sense of community and increases trust.

Leadership entails:

The ability to guide, motivate, and provide team members the autonomy they need to achieve their full potential is essential to effective team leadership. Strong leadership helps to foster a common vision among members of the team and gives the required direction for moving the group closer to accomplishing its objectives.

Taking Responsibility:

Every member of the team needs to accept personal accountability for their deeds and responsibilities. By ensuring that tasks are finished on time and at the desired standard, accountability contributes to the overall performance of the team.

The Importance of Working Together:

Reaching Our Shared Objectives:

To accomplish group goals and aims that would be challenging to accomplish on an individual basis, efficient collaboration among team members is absolutely necessary. Teams are able to execute difficult tasks in a more expedient and successful manner when they capitalize on the skills of each individual member of the team.

Invention and Creative Problem Solving:

Working together as a team frequently results in the development of original ideas and approaches. When people who come from different backgrounds and have varying areas of expertise collaborate, they have the potential to come up with novel and unconventional solutions to problems.

Enhanced Capability to Solve Problems:

Through collaborative brainstorming and analytical thought, teams can more effectively tackle difficult problems. The varied perspectives and points of view that members of a team bring to the table can help lead to solutions that are comprehensive and well-rounded.

Productivity Gains as a Result of:

A productive work environment is directly correlated to strong teamwork. Teams are able to finish projects more quickly and with a greater degree of quality when they divide up the work and capitalize on the capabilities of each individual member of the team.

Development both Personally and Professionally:

Individual progress and advancement can be facilitated by participation in a productive team environment. The members of the team have the opportunity to improve their abilities, increase their knowledge, and build their professional networks by working together and learning from one another.

Comprehending the Meaning of Social Bonding:

Believe :

Strong social relationships are built on a solid foundation of trust. To earn someone's trust, you need to be honest, have integrity, and be reliable. You also need to create an atmosphere in which individuals can feel safe and secure inside the group.

Respect on Both Sides:

It is absolutely necessary to show respect for one another's thoughts, points of view, and contributions if one want to cultivate strong social ties. A social environment that is harmonious and welcoming to people of many backgrounds and perspectives can be fostered by recognizing and appreciating the value of diversity.

Compassion :

It is essential to develop empathy and an understanding of the feelings and experiences of others in order to successfully form strong social ties. A community that is compassionate, supporting, and caring is one that has a strong foundation in empathy.

Values and Objectives That Are Shared:

Having a feeling of purpose in common with others and holding similar values might help to strengthen social relationships. When individuals match their goals with the goals of the group as a whole, they experience feelings of togetherness and a sense of belonging inside the group.

Communication that is fruitful:

For the purpose of cultivating social relationships, it is essential to communicate in an open, positive, and courteous manner. Meaningful connections and a sense of camaraderie can be fostered through practices such as active listening and good communication.

The Importance of Forming Relationships with Others:

A Feeling of Complementarity:

A community or group can foster a sense of acceptance and belonging through the development of strong social relationships. People have the impression that they are valued and supported, which results in a social setting that is constructive and welcoming to everybody.

Support on an Emotional Level:

During difficult times, the emotional support provided by social bonds is invaluable. Having a

a supporting network of friends and coworkers helps individuals cope with stress and adversity, which in turn builds resilience in those who possess such a network.

The state of one's mind:

The development of strong social relationships has been related to an increase in one's mental health. The ability to have happy, meaningful relationships as well as a sense of overall connection all play a part in one's level of happiness and overall satisfaction with life.

Enhanced Working Relationships and Cooperation:

Individuals are more likely to work together and cooperate when they have strong social bonds. When people have the sense that they are connected to others and valued, there is a greater likelihood that they will work together amicably and accomplish success as a group.

Integrity of the Community:

The cohesion and peace of a society are aided by the existence of strong social relationships. A community that is cohesive cultivates a sense of unity, a common purpose, and mutual respect, which ultimately results in a social environment that is more dynamic and supportive.

Methods for Fostering Productive Cooperation Within Teams and Stronger Social Bonds

Create an Atmosphere That Is Uplifting And Accepting:

Establish a culture that welcomes open communication, acknowledges the value of different points of view, and places a premium on the contributions made by all members of the team.

Clearly define both your goals and your expectations:

Establish crystal-clear objectives and standards for the team, making it a point to ensure that every member is aware of the part they play and the responsibilities they bear in the pursuit of these goals.

Activities that encourage collaboration and building teams should be encouraged:

It is important to organize events and initiatives that encourage members of a team to work together, create trust in one another, and engage in social interaction with one another.

Make available opportunities for the growth and development of skills:

It is important to provide members of the team with chances for training and development so that they can improve their abilities, increase their knowledge, and more effectively contribute to the success of the team.

Honoring Accomplishments and Important Milestones

A sense of pride and success can be fostered among team members by publicly acknowledging and celebrating the group's accomplishments and milestones.

Encourage communication that is both open and respectful:

Encourage an environment of communication that is both open and respectful, one in which members of the team may feel at ease expressing their thoughts, concerns, and comments without worrying that they will be judged.

Encourage the Development of a Culture Based on Compassion and Understanding:

Encourage members of the team to understand one another and show empathy for one another in order to foster an environment that is helpful and empathetic.

Setting a Good Example:

You should demonstrate great leadership characteristics for the team by cultivating a culture of respect and boosting collaborative efforts and teamwork. This will set a good example for the rest of the team.

Develop your social connections and network of resources to help you:

Help members of the team create strong social relationships and support networks by facilitating opportunities for them to interact with one another socially and engage in networking.

Encourage a Sense of Purpose and the Development of Shared Values:

It is important to clearly communicate the purpose of the team as well as its values, with an emphasis on the significance of individual contributions to the team's overall performance and the good effects of working toward common objectives.

3.3 Focus, concentration, and decision-making

In this day and age, where there are continual distractions and an abundance of information, the ability to maintain focus, concentration, and make sound decisions is an absolutely necessary talent. These mental operations are necessary for success in many facets of life, ranging from one's personal productivity to their professional accomplishments. In the course of this in-depth investigation, we dive into the significance of focus, concentration, and decision-making, as well as their impact on performance and the tactics and practices that might develop these crucial cognitive capacities.

Recognizing the Importance of Concentration, Focus, and Decision-Making: On this:

The mental capacity to direct one's attention and energy toward a particular activity, purpose, or objective while disregarding distractions is what we mean when we talk about focus. Concentration is the process of focusing one's attention on a particular idea, activity, or area of interest to the exclusion of all other stimuli.

Focusing one's attention:

The mental effort and attention that must be maintained over time in order to carry out a task or participate in an activity is an essential component of concentration, which is closely related to focus. It requires a profound and unyielding dedication to the here and now.

Formulation of Decisions:

The mental process of selecting one course of action among a number of possible future outcomes, often known as options or alternatives, is referred to as decision-making. It entails making a judgment or choice after evaluating the facts, thinking about the outcomes that could result from each option, and so on.

The Importance of Maintaining Focus and Concentration While Making Decisions:

Productivity that is Greater:

Productivity can be considerably increased by improving one's capacity to focus and concentrate efficiently. People have a tendency to finish tasks more quickly and effectively when they are able to concentrate on the task at hand without being interrupted.

Workmanlike Qualities:

Maintaining one's concentration throughout a work guarantees that it will be completed with accuracy and consideration for the smallest of details. When decisions are made with full attention, the results are marked by improved quality both in the choices and the outcomes.

Creative Problem-Solving and Thinking Outside the Box:

It is easier to come up with original ideas if one is able to concentrate their thoughts on a particular challenge or creative endeavor. Concentration is the finest way to foster creative thinking, while decision-making guarantees that the most valuable ideas are chosen.

Management of One's Time:

Individuals are able to prioritize work, allot time efficiently, and keep themselves on track when they make decisions that are effective. This enables effective management of time as well as the completion of tasks.

Relaxation Techniques:

Concentration and attention that is focused on the work at hand can help alleviate stress by minimizing the influence of extraneous distractions and establishing a sense of control over the activity that is being performed. The anxiety that is linked with not knowing something can also be reduced by effective decision-making.

Development both Personally and Professionally:

Acquiring new skills, expanding one's knowledge base, and making progress in one's job are all products of being able to concentrate on one's own personal and professional development. The ability to make decisions that are effective assists individuals in selecting choices that are congruent with their objectives.

Techniques for Improving One's Ability to Focus, Concentrate, and Make Decisions:

Meditation with Attention to the Present:

Training the mind to pay attention to what is happening in the here and now while letting go of whatever is distracting can be accomplished through mindfulness meditation. Focus and concentration can be improved via consistent practice.

Optimization of the Environment:

Establish a setting that encourages concentration on the task at hand. Reduce the number of things that can divert your attention, keep your workstation clear of clutter, and utilize noise-cancelling headphones or other equipment to shut out any outside interruptions.

Establishing Priorities for Work:

Determine which activities are most important to focus on by making use of tools for task prioritization, such as the Eisenhower Matrix. This guarantees that the task that is most important gets the appropriate attention that it requires.

Techniques for Managing One's Time

Utilize methods for managing time such as the Pomodoro Technique, which consists of intense work times followed by brief breaks. This strategy may help enhance concentration as well as the ability to make decisions.

A break from technology:

In order to reduce the amount of time wasted due to digital distractions, it is recommended to schedule "digital detox" periods in which activities such as checking email and participating in social media are prohibited. This is a skill that can help improve concentration as well as decision-making.

Exercising and Maintaining a Healthy Body:

The ability to think clearly and solve problems is improved by engaging in regular physical activity and taking care of one's health. Physical activity improves focus and attention by increasing the volume of blood that flows to the brain.

Sleeping and relaxing:

It is imperative that you get enough sleep and relax, as both are necessary for proper cognitive performance. The inability to get enough sleep might make it difficult to concentrate, focus, and make decisions.

Setting Objectives:

Create goals that are both short-term and long-term that are crystal obvious and can be accomplished. Goals make it simpler to concentrate on the activities that are important because they provide both direction and a sense of purpose.

Mapping the Mind:

The visual depiction of ideas and concepts that is known as mind mapping. It helps individuals see the wider picture while organizing their thoughts, which in turn makes it easier for them to make decisions.

Talking to Oneself Favorably:

Boosting one's self-confidence and improving one's ability to make decisions can be accomplished by cultivating positive self-talk and affirmations. The ability to make decisions with less reluctance is facilitated by having confidence in one's own capabilities.

Alternatives to Unhealthy Lifestyles:

Eat a well-rounded diet, don't let yourself get dehydrated, and steer clear of drinking too much coffee or alcohol. Cognitive functions and mental clarity are both supported by leading a healthy lifestyle.

Learning That Never Stops:

Continuous learning is a great way to keep your mind busy, as well as to test and improve your cognitive abilities. The ability to concentrate and make decisions can be improved via the acquisition of new knowledge and abilities.

Activities for the Mind:

Participate in cerebral activities such as puzzles, brain games, and training to improve your memory. The cognitive skills can be honed and concentration can be improved through these activities.

Consideration of Oneself and Reflection:

Consider the decisions you've made and how they've turned out from time to time. Learning from one's own experiences and drawing conclusions based on those memories is one of the primary benefits of engaging in self-evaluation.

Networks of Assistance:

Seek the support of mentors, peers, or coaches who are able to provide direction and insights into effective decision-making and ask for their assistance. The ability to make decisions jointly can often result in improved options.

The cognitive abilities of focus, concentration, and decision-making are intricately intertwined, and together they constitute the foundation of efficient performance in many different facets of life. These qualities are essential for accomplishing a variety of objectives, including completing activities, finding solutions to difficulties, and realizing personal and professional goals. Individuals can not only improve their productivity and the quality of their work by adopting techniques and practices to enhance these cognitive functions, but they can also reduce their stress and make more well-informed decisions as a result of doing so. The cultivation of abilities such as focus, concentration, and the ability to make sound decisions is, in the end, an investment in one's own personal growth and the key to realizing one's full potential.

3.4 Leadership and responsibility

Leadership is more than just a position of authority; it is the obligation to guide and inspire people towards a common purpose. Leadership is more than just a position of authority. Integrity, accountability, and a dedication to serving a purpose higher than oneself are the defining characteristics of effective leadership. Leaders take on the duty of making decisions that have an effect on their teams, companies, and communities. They also have the obligation to put the health and development of those who follow their leadership as a top priority. Leaders have the ability to cultivate trust, propel positive change, and establish a culture that values cooperation and accomplishment when they take ownership of their responsibilities.

Leadership with Honesty and Integrity:

The foundation of strong leadership is honesty and moral rectitude. Honesty, ethical decision-making, and consistency in one's actions and words are all qualities that leaders are expected to exhibit. Leaders are able to acquire the trust and respect of their teams and cultivate an environment that is transparent and real when they continue to uphold a strong moral compass.

Holding Oneself Responsible and Taking Ownership:

Leaders are expected to accept full responsibility for their deeds and choices. It is absolutely necessary to accept responsibility for both one's accomplishments and one's shortcomings in order to develop trust and credibility. A culture of responsibility and growth may be fostered when leaders set an example for their teams by taking responsibility for their own actions and encouraging others to do the same.

Using One's Vision and Purpose as a Compass:

Leaders who are effective are able to motivate their followers by presenting a crystal clear vision and goal. Leaders are able to drive their teams to strive for greatness and to contribute to a common goal when they communicate a mission that is both captivating and attainable. A sense of purpose and the ability to nurture a cohesive and motivated team can be cultivated through the provision of guidance and direction that is founded on a solid vision.

Giving Agency to Third Parties:

A competent leader delegated authority to their team members, giving them the resources, support, and autonomy they required to achieve success in their endeavors. Leaders provide their teams the opportunity to take ownership of their work and make a positive contribution to the organization's success when they cultivate an environment based on trust and delegating. The empowerment of others not only propels the progress of the individual, but also improves the performance of the team and the total productivity.

Acceptance of Difference and Participation:

Respecting different perspectives and include everyone are essential components of responsible leadership, both inside the team and the company. Leaders may establish a culture of respect and collaboration by cultivating an atmosphere that recognizes the contributions of individuals with varying viewpoints, experiences, and backgrounds. The acceptance of diverse viewpoints and experiences boosts the inventiveness, creativity, and overall performance of a team.

Motivating and Fostering Positive Change:

Leaders who exercise responsibility can serve as agents of constructive change. They push for ongoing development, innovation, and adaptation to the ever-changing difficulties that face society. Leaders may inspire their people to accept change and look for possibilities for growth and progress when they foster a culture that values learning and development and encourages its spread.

3.5 Coping with pressure and resilience

Individuals frequently experience significant amounts of pressure and stress in their personal lives as well as in their professional life due to the fast-paced and demanding nature of the society we live in today. Individuals may traverse problems, bounce back from setbacks, and prosper in the face of adversity by developing key abilities such as coping with pressure and nurturing resilience. These talents help individuals to manage challenges. Individuals are able to effectively handle stress, preserve mental well-being, and accomplish achievement even in the most trying settings if they acquire good coping skills and build resilience.

Recognizing the Role of Pressure and Resilience:

The force of:

When people are placed in circumstances that are difficult or demanding, they often experience

sensations of stress and tension, which are collectively referred to as pressure. It doesn't matter if it's looming work deadlines, mounting personal commitments, or unanticipated roadblocks: pressure may take many forms and have a negative effect on both mental and physical health.

Resistance to fracturing:

The capacity to adjust to and recover from adversity, trauma, or extreme stress is what we mean when we talk about resilience. People who are resilient are able to display emotional fortitude, tenacity, and the ability to triumph over challenges and failures, emerging from the experience stronger and more capable than they were before.

Methods for Defending Against the Effects of Pressure:

Management of One's Time:

Effective time management helps individuals prioritize tasks, create realistic goals, and allocate time for both work and personal interests. This strategy lessens the sensation of being overpowered and enables individuals to better regulate the effects of pressure on their bodies.

Techniques for the Reduction of Stress:

Individuals who engage in stress-reduction strategies such as deep breathing, meditation, or mindfulness practices may find that they are better able to manage their stress levels and keep a sense of calm even when they are confronted with situations that are fraught with pressure.

Exercices of a Physical Nature:

Exerting oneself physically on a consistent basis is beneficial not just to one's physical health but also to one's mental and emotional well-being. Endorphins, which are released during exercise, can help boost mood and lower stress, making it a healthy and effective approach to deal with strain.

Communication That Is Effective:

When it comes to pressure management, open and effective communication is absolutely necessary. Relieving stress and providing a sense of relaxation can be accomplished by voicing concerns, seeking support, and discussing one's experiences with trustworthy individuals.

Having Expectations That Are Realistic:

Managing pressure involves lowering the demand for perfection, which can be accomplished by setting more reasonable standards for oneself and others. The load of strain can be lightened by gaining an awareness that it is acceptable to make errors and that not everything has to be perfect at all times.

Techniques for the Development of Resilience:

Think of the Bright Side:

Strengthening one's ability to bounce back from adversity can be accomplished by practicing optimism and looking for the bright side of difficult circumstances. Thinking positively instills a person with a sense of hope and optimism, which in turn enables them to face challenges head-on and with a sense of determination.

The Management of Emotions:

Individuals who develop their skills in emotional regulation are able to properly regulate and cope with a wide range of powerful emotions. Having the ability to identify, comprehend, and exercise control over one's feelings helps one to become more resilient and improves one's overall well-being.

Abilities in Problem Solving:

Individuals are able to approach issues in a more effective manner if they have improved their problem-solving skills. Individuals can cultivate resilience and approach challenges with confidence if they first break down problems into steps that are more manageable and then look for practical answers to those steps.

Assistance from Others:

During trying times, having a strong support network consisting of friends, family, and coworkers may be an invaluable source of both emotional support and guidance. Individuals are given a sense of belonging and connection through the provision of social support, which in turn helps to promote resilience.

Capacity for Adaptation and Flexibility:

Individuals can more quickly adjust to changes and unexpected events if they have developed their adaptability and flexibility through deliberate practice. Being resilient requires individuals to be open to new experiences, ideas, and ways of thinking. This opens the door for individuals to handle uncertainty with resilience.

Techniques for Thriving When You're Under Pressure and Building Your Resilience:

The Practices of Mindfulness:

Developing one's capacity for resilience and lessening the toll that stress takes on mental health can be accomplished by participating in mindfulness practices such as meditation and yoga. These activities can help individuals remain grounded and present.

Continuous Efforts Towards Learning and Progress:

The development of resiliency can be aided by cultivating a sense of curiosity, adaptability, and a readiness to take on new challenges and opportunities. Adopting a growth mindset and embracing continuous learning are two ways to do this.

Developing Your Own Self-Confidence:

Individuals are able to confront issues with a sense of competence and assurance once they have developed their self-confidence and self-efficacy via personal development. Increasing one's level of self-confidence not only helps promote resilience but also gives individuals the strength to confront challenges with tenacity and determination.

Adopting Positive Methods of Dealing with Stress:

Developing resilience and the ability to preserve mental and emotional well-being in the face of adversity is made easier when individuals steer clear of unhealthy coping methods such as substance misuse and escapism and instead choose healthy coping strategies.

Creating a Workplace That Is Comfortable And Supportive:

It is crucial to create a supportive work environment that prioritizes work-life balance, open communication, and the overall well-being of employees in order to promote resilience and enable workers to thrive in an atmosphere that is high in pressure.

Individuals may effectively manage pressure, overcome problems, and thrive in even the most challenging environments if they develop resilience and put into practice good coping mechanisms. These tactics not only build a sense of mental well-being, but they also cultivate a sense of empowerment and capability, which enables individuals to accomplish both personal and professional success in spite of the stresses of modern life.

Chapter 4

The Power of Community

The significance of community cannot be emphasized in a world that is always evolving and increasingly linked. Communities play an essential part in building connection, offering support, and stimulating collective growth. This is true whether the community in question is a physical neighborhood, an online forum, or a group that shares a common interest. The strength of a community comes in its capacity to bring people together, foster a sense of belonging among its members, and encourage collaboration and mutual help among its members. We dive into the relevance of community, the influence of communal assistance, and the different ways in which communities contribute to personal, social, and global growth in this in-depth investigation.

Comprehending the Meaning of Community:
The following is a definition of community:

A community can be defined as a collection of persons who support one another, share resources, and work to develop a sense of belonging by having common interests, goals, or experiences and coming together to support and encourage one another. Communities can take many different forms, including geographical communities, virtual communities, and communities based on similar views or ideals. Some communities even exist in both physical and virtual spaces.

Components That Make Up a Thriving Community

A sense of belonging, mutual support, shared values, and a dedication to the collective well-being are the distinguishing characteristics of healthy communities. They make it possible for individuals to connect with one another, work together, and contribute to the greater welfare of the community.

The Importance of Belonging to a Community
A Feeling of Complementarity:

A sense of belonging and connectedness can be fostered through community, which also provides individuals with a network of support and a setting in which they can discuss their experiences, difficulties, and successes.

Support for Emotional Needs and a Sense of Well-Being:
During times of distress, communities provide emotional support by offering comfort, empathy, and compassion to those who are suffering. Having friends and neighbors who care about you can do wonders for your mental and emotional health.

Preserving Cultural Authenticity While Maintaining Identity:
Communities play an essential part in the maintenance of cultural history and identity, as well as in the development of a sense of pride and belonging among the people who make up those communities.

Maintaining social harmony and cohesion:
Strong communities foster social cohesiveness and harmony, helping to bridge the gap between various groups of people while also cultivating understanding, tolerance, and respect.

Working Together and Taking Collective Action:
Individuals are able to work together towards common goals, whether they be related to social, environmental, or economic challenges, when communities foster collaboration and collective action.

The Effects of Having Support from Your Community:
Growth and development on a personal level:
Individuals are provided with mentorship, advice, and resources for self-improvement and skill enhancement when they have access to the communal support that is available to them. This encourages personal growth and development.

Opportunities for Professional Networking and Participation:
Communities provide individuals with valuable chances for professional networking by linking them with other professionals who share their interests, with mentors, and with possible employers or collaborators.

Learning Together and the Free Flow of Information:
People are able to gain access to a wider range of viewpoints, experiences, and areas of expertise when they are part of communities because these communities enable shared learning and the exchange of knowledge.

Advocacy and the Promotion of Empowerment:
Individuals gain the ability to advocate for their rights and interests, which amplifies their voices
and drives positive change in their communities and societies when they have the backing of their communities.

Assistance to One Another and a Sense of Reciprocity:
Individuals are able to support one another within communities because there is a culture of mutual assistance and reciprocity. This culture encourages individuals to support one another by sharing resources, providing direction, and offering assistance when it is required.

The Importance of Communities to One's Own, Society's, and the World's Overall Development:

Personal growth and overall health and happiness:
Individuals receive the emotional support, resources for growth, and opportunities for self-expression and fulfillment that they need from their communities, which in turn contributes to the individual's overall development and well-being.

Integration and Inclusion of All Social Groups:
Communities create social integration and inclusivity by developing gathering places where people from a variety of backgrounds may interact with one another, exchange their
perspectives, and work to deepen their mutual respect and understanding.

Engagement in Public Life and Participation:
Individuals are motivated to take an active position in community activities, social issues, and advocacy efforts when communities encourage civic engagement and involvement and provide opportunities for individuals to get involved.

Empowering People Economically and Promoting Sustainable Development:
The economic empowerment of individuals and the promotion of sustainable practices are two of the most important roles that communities can play. Communities may play these roles by encouraging entrepreneurship, offering employment opportunities, and advocating for sustainable practices.

Assistance to Humanitarian Causes Around the World:
The mobilization of resources, the promotion of awareness, and the provision of support to communities and persons in need, regardless of geographical limits, are all contributions that global communities make to the cause of global solidarity and humanitarian relief.

Methods for Constructing Communities That Are Solid And Helpful:
Fostering Inclusion and Respect for Diversity:
Encourage a community-wide culture that values inclusiveness and diversity by extending a warm welcome to individuals who come from a variety of experiences, backgrounds, and points of view.

Creating an Open Communication Environment:
Establish means of open communication and dialogue within the community, and encourage its members to actively participate, share their thoughts, and provide feedback that is constructive.

Facilitating the Growth of Community Leaders:
It is important to empower community leaders by providing them with the tools and assistance they need to steer the community toward the achievement of shared objectives and the promotion of good change.

Opportunities for Collaboration Are Created Through:
In order to inspire people of the community to work together towards common goals and to foster a sense of togetherness and collaboration, it is important to organize community-wide collaborative projects, events, and initiatives.

Offering Access to Necessary Resources and Assistance:

Provide community members with access to resources, support services, and educational opportunities that contribute to their personal and professional growth.

Creating a Society That Encourages Empathy and Compassion:

It is important to promote empathy and compassion within a community in order to foster an environment that is caring and supportive, one in which individuals can feel understood, appreciated, and respected.

Honoring the Richness and Diversity of Our Cultural Heritage:

Fostering a sense of pride and individuality, as well as a sense of collective pride, among the members of the community can be accomplished through the planning and execution of cultural activities, such as festivals, celebrations, and events.

Fostering Environmental Consciousness and the Adoption of Sustainable Practices:

Encourage projects that contribute to the preservation of the environment and the development of eco-friendly lifestyles, and advocate for sustainable practices and environmental awareness within the community.

Developing Strategic Alliances and Working Relationships:

Fostering a network of support and collaboration for community development can be accomplished by establishing partnerships and collaborations with other communities, organizations, and institutions that have values and goals that are comparable to your own.

Advancing Education and Instruction That Lasts a Lifetime:

Place an emphasis on education and the pursuit of lifelong learning within the community, and ensure that members have access to educational programs, workshops, and other training opportunities that will aid in their personal development as well as the development of the group as a whole.

The ability of a community to facilitate connection, support, and collective development is the source of its strength. Communities have the potential to play a significant role in the personal, social, and global development of individuals by encouraging inclusivity, encouraging open communication, and offering access to resources and support. Communities serve as the foundational element in the process of building unity, empowerment, and good change. This can occur through the provision of emotional support, through collaborative activities, or through advocacy efforts. Individuals have the ability to create a society that is more connected, inclusive, and resilient by recognizing and embracing the power of community. This type of society is one that fosters the well-being and progress of its people.

4.1 The role of cricket clubs and organizations

Cricket has a long and illustrious history, and its continued popularity is due in large part to the efforts of numerous clubs and organizations. These organizations serve as the backbone of the cricketing world in a variety of capacities, including the development of talent, the promotion of a passion for the game, the development of a feeling of community, and the provision of platforms for competitive play. In this in-depth investigation, we look into the complex role that cricket clubs and organizations play, their impact on the game and the community, as well as the numerous projects and programs that cricket clubs and organizations do to support the development and achievement of cricket at all different levels.

Fostering Skill Acquisition and Development of Talent:

Programs for the Development of Young People:

Cricket clubs and organizations frequently undertake youth development programs with the goal of spotting and fostering young talent in the sport. Aspiring young cricketers can participate in these programs to receive coaching, training, and opportunities to compete, all of which help to nurture both the development of cricketing skills and an early-on interest for the sport.

Training facilities such as academies and camps:

In the sport of cricket, numerous organizations and clubs provide specialized academies and training camps where participants can receive extensive coaching, improve their skills, and receive mentoring from seasoned experts. These programs are of critical importance in developing the talents of aspiring players and preparing them for higher levels of competitive cricket.

Identifying Potential and Scouting for Talent:

Cricket clubs and organizations run talent identification and scouting programs in order to locate and solicit applications from talented players hailing from a variety of backgrounds. These activities contribute to the development of a talent pipeline, which ensures a consistent flow of quality players into the ecosystem of cricket.

Increasing Participation in, and Openness to, the Community:

Outreach to the Local Community:

Cricket clubs regularly engage with the communities in which they are located by arranging events, workshops, and outreach initiatives to promote the sport and encourage involvement among individuals of all ages and backgrounds. These initiatives contribute to the community's development of a sense of inclusiveness as well as unity.

Partnerships Between Schools and Colleges:

Cricket clubs and organizations that collaborate with educational institutions are able to offer the sport of cricket to students and encourage active engagement from those students. Cricket clubs make significant contributions to the general development of the sport at the grassroots level by cultivating ties with educational institutions like schools and colleges.

Encouragement of Diverse Opinions and Inclusion:

Emphasizing diversity and inclusion, cricket clubs and organizations strive to create an environment that welcomes individuals from all walks of life. These organizations contribute to the expansion and enrichment of the cricketing community through the promotion of diversity. In doing so, they help to develop a culture that values respect and unity.

Making Competitive Platforms and Tournaments More Easily Accessible:

Organizing Tournaments at the Local and Regional Levels:
Cricket clubs and organizations play an important role in the organization of local and regional
competitions, which give players the opportunity to gain valuable experience competing against their peers. The purpose of these competitions is to provide athletes with opportunities to display their talents, encourage the development of healthy competition, and encourage good sportsmanship.

The Hosting of Events on a National and International Scale:
The most prominent cricket clubs and organizations regularly play host to national as well as international competitions, which helps to further the sport's development and raises its profile on a global scale. These competitions bring together some of the best players in the world, showing the highest level of cricket while also fostering cross-cultural understanding and togetherness.

The Provision of Necessary Facilities and Infrastructure:
Cricket clubs and organizations make investments in the development of cutting-edge infrastructure and facilities. These investments can include the upkeep of grounds, the construction of training facilities, and the addition of contemporary amenities. These facilities act as focal points for many aspects of cricket and contribute to the development and continued viability of the sport as a whole.

Fostering Good Sportsmanship and Honorable Behavior:
Promoting Honesty and Fair Play while Maintaining Integrity:
Clubs and associations dedicated to the sport of cricket encourage its participants, coaches, and officials to uphold the ideals of fair play, sportsmanship, and ethical behavior. These organizations help to ensure that cricket continues to be played in an environment that is robust and competitive by promoting principles of honesty and decency within the sport.

Policies Regarding the Prohibition of Doping and a Code of Conduct:
A significant number of cricket clubs and organizations uphold stringent anti-doping regulations and a code of conduct that stresses the significance of preserving a clean and ethical approach to the sport. These policies contribute, on a broad scale, to the honesty and legitimacy of the sport of cricket.

Fostering the Development of Cricket as a Full-Fledged Professional Sport:
Improvements Made to Professional Leagues:
Cricket clubs and organizations play a crucial part in the formation and maintenance of professional cricket leagues, which give players with lucrative opportunities and platforms for showing their skills on a worldwide stage. These leagues are managed by individuals who are responsible for the construction of the leagues. The marketing and internationalization of the sport is facilitated by the existence of these leagues.

Player Assistance and Professionalization Programs:
Cricket clubs and organizations make the welfare and development of players a top priority. To this end, they provide players with support programs, financial incentives,

and other tools to assist them in reaching their full potential in the game. These programs contribute to the overall health and growth of cricket players, as well as their professional development.

Participating in Activities With a Positive Social Impact and Community Service:

Programs with a Charitable Focus and a Focus on Social Impact:

Cricket clubs and organizations frequently get involved in philanthropic and social impact projects with the goals of giving back to the society and tackling various social issues. These programs help individuals and communities in disadvantaged situations improve their circumstances and gain more control over their lives.

Encouragement of Physical and Emotional Health and Well-Being:

Numerous cricket clubs and organizations support health and well-being projects that encourage active engagement in sports, healthy living choices, and physical fitness. Some of these initiatives are included below. These activities contribute to the overall improvement of public health and wellness within the community, which is a result of the overall improvement of public health.

An Argument in Favor of the Expansion and Recognizance of Women's Cricket:

Supporting the Development of Cricket for Women:

Cricket clubs and organizations actively push for the expansion and recognition of women's

cricket by creating specific programs, tournaments, and initiatives that assist the development of women cricketers at all levels. This is done in order to encourage more women to participate in cricket. These activities help to the empowerment of women in the sport as well as increasing their visibility.

Programs to Promote Gender Equality and Inclusivity:

Cricket clubs and organizations advocate efforts to encourage the active engagement of women in cricket and create a more inclusive and diverse landscape of cricketing, putting an emphasis on the importance of gender equality and inclusivity in the sport.

4.2 Building a supportive and inclusive cricket community

Cricket, like any other sport, flourishes when it embraces diversity and inclusivity, and when it does so in a way that creates an atmosphere in which all individuals feel welcome and cherished. Not only does the presence of a welcoming and accepting cricket community generate a sense of belonging, but it also promotes individual development and good sportsmanship. In the course of this in-depth investigation, we dig into the relevance of constructing a cricket community that is both supportive and inclusive, the influence it has on individuals and the sport, as well as the methods and activities that contribute to the expansion of this community.

Comprehending the Meaning of Inclusivity in Cricket:

Definition of Inclusivity:

In cricket, the concept of "inclusivity" refers to the practice of cultivating an atmosphere in which players of any and every background, gender, ability, and age can participate, contribute, and enjoy the sport without being subjected to discrimination or being excluded from it.

Why It's So Important to Be Inclusive:

For the sport of cricket to continue to thrive and expand, inclusivity is very necessary. It guarantees that the sport will continue to be relevant, that it will reach a larger audience, and that it will benefit from a diverse range of viewpoints and talents.

The Importance of Creating a Community That Is Both Supportive and Inclusive in Cricket:

Creating a Stronger Sense of Community by:

A cricket community that is welcoming, accepting, and supporting cultivates a sense of belonging and unity, which enables all members to experience feelings of being respected and appreciated. This, in turn, motivates individuals to maintain their involvement in the activity and their passion for it.

Growth and development on a personal level:

Individuals have the opportunity to develop not only their cricketing talents but also essential life skills such as teamwork, leadership, and communication when they are in an environment that is welcoming to all. Regardless of one's history or level of experience, it can serve as a foundation for one's own personal development.

Improving Sportsmanship through:

Fair play, respect for opponents, and ethical behavior are all encouraged within an inclusive cricket society. It contributes to the general integrity and reputation of the sport by fostering a culture of sportsmanship and providing an incentive for good sportsmanship.

Expanding One's Circumference of Influence:

Cricket is able to broaden its appeal to a wider range of cultures and demographics if it welcomes players from all walks of life. This helps to ensure cricket's ongoing development and sustained relevance in today's rapidly changing globe.

Strategies for Constructing a Community That Is Both Supportive and Inclusive to All Cricket Players:

Instruction in and sensitivity to diversity:

Cricket organizations must to offer diversity training and awareness programs to their members in order to assist members in gaining an understanding of the significance of inclusivity and in recognizing and resolving issues connected to bias, discrimination, and exclusion.

Guaranteeing Everyone the Same Chances:

Make sure that everyone, regardless of gender, age, ethnicity, or ability, has equal access to opportunities for playing, coaching, and officiating, and that these opportunities are treated similarly. Adopt some new policies that will help further the cause of gender equality and inclusiveness.

Participation in the Community and Efforts to Reach Out:
Cricket clubs and organizations can get involved with the communities in which they are located by contacting local institutions of higher education, social groups, and schools in order to introduce them to the sport of cricket. Programs designed to reach out to the community can help remove barriers and encourage new involvement.

Easy and Reasonable Access:
Create additional opportunities for people to participate in cricket by lowering the cost of programs, gear, and facilities. This opens up the opportunity for people from a wide variety of socioeconomic levels to compete in the sport.

Assistance and guidance are provided:
Develop mentoring programs that pair seasoned players, coaches, or officials with beginners, providing the latter with advice and assistance as they navigate the sport. This mentoring program can assist newcomers in acclimating to the sport of cricket as well as the community that surrounds it.

The importance of cultural sensitivity and acceptance:
Celebrate a variety of cultural events, customs, and practices within the community of cricket players, and use this opportunity to promote cultural understanding and acceptance. Recognize and appreciate the many different people who participate in cricket.

Playing Formats That Are Adaptable:
Provide a variety of game types as well as different divisions to play in so that players of varying skill levels and time commitments can participate. More people will be able to participate in the sport if the rules are flexible enough to accommodate their individual tastes.

Programs That Are Inclusive of Both Sexes
Create gender-inclusive cricket programs that cater to the special requirements and preferences of female participants, with the goal of increasing the number of women who participate actively in the sport of cricket.

Ability to be reached:
Make sure that those with disabilities may easily access the cricket facilities so that they can take part in the sport and enjoy it without any restrictions.

Policies that Seek to Eliminate Discrimination:
In the cricket community, it is imperative that stringent anti-discrimination regulations be strictly enforced. These laws should forbid any and all forms of discrimination as well as harassment. The adoption of these policies sends a loud and unambiguous statement that inclusion is a value that cannot be negotiated.

Mechanisms for Providing Feedback:
Create feedback tools that give members of the community the opportunity to express their concerns or make suggestions regarding how inclusivity and support may be improved. This encourages openness of information and accountability.

The following are examples of initiatives and programs that promote inclusivity:

Campaigns for the Game of Cricket for All:

Create initiatives like "Cricket for All" that highlight the value of diversity and encourage people from all walks of life to take part in the sport.

Festivals of Cricket in the Community:

Community cricket festivals should be organized so that people of all walks of life can come together to talk about their shared passion for the sport and compete against one another in a spirit of goodwill.

Outreach Programs for Young People:

Create youth outreach activities that highlight the ideals of teamwork, respect, and inclusivity while introducing cricket to a younger audience.

Multiple Officiating and Coaching Panels to Choose From:

Make sure that the people serving on the coaching and officiating panels come from a wide variety of ethnicities and genders. Aspiring coaches and officials can learn from these diverse examples and take advantage of the opportunities they present.

Tournaments and Leagues That Are Open to Everyone:

Initiate cricket competitions and leagues that are open to all players, including those who are unable to play or have other requirements, and that actively seek out and welcome their participation.

Initiatives for Women Who Play Cricket:

Whether at the grass-roots or the professional level, you should encourage and promote programs that highlight and support the participation of women in cricket.

4.3 The impact of mentors and coaches

Mentors and coaches serve a critical role in directing individuals towards personal and professional progress by providing them with essential support, expertise, and encouragement. This is because mentors and coaches play a key role in helping individuals towards growth. Mentors and coaches can act as trusted advisors and role models for individuals in a variety of settings, including athletics, academics, and personal development. They can assist individuals in reaching their full potential by providing them with direction, inspiration, and constructive feedback. In the course of this in-depth investigation, we dive into the enormous impact that mentors and coaches have, their influence on the development of skills and the personal empowerment of mentees, as well as the many tactics and approaches that mentors and coaches use to motivate and encourage those they work with.

Acquiring an Understanding of the Role That Mentors and Coaches Play: Role Models:

Mentors are more experienced individuals who work with less experienced individuals to provide direction, knowledge, and support in order to assist those individuals in overcoming problems, making more informed decisions, and accomplishing their goals.

The Trainers:

Coaches are professionals that help people or teams acquire specific abilities, enhance performance, and achieve success in their chosen field or discipline by providing them with specialized training, teaching, and feedback. Coaches may work in a variety of fields and disciplines.

The Importance of Role Models, Mentors, and Coaches:

Personalized Assistance in the Form of Advice and Support:

Mentors and coaches provide their mentees with individualized direction and support that is catered to meet the specific requirements and goals of each mentee. This tailored approach helps to cultivate a deep link between individuals and provides an environment that is beneficial to both personal and professional growth.

Development of Skills and Improvement of Performance:

Mentors and coaches help individuals gain new capabilities, hone current talents, and overcome constraints or restrictions by virtue of the expertise and information that they bring to the table in their roles as facilitators of skill growth and refinement.

Support on an Emotional and Motivational Level:

The emotional and motivational support that mentors and coaches provide to their mentees helps to enhance their self-confidence and resiliency, which is especially beneficial during trying times or when confronted with obstacles.

Feedback That Is Helpful and Critical Thinking:

Mentors and coaches help individuals recognize their strengths and weaknesses by providing constructive criticism and evaluation. They also encourage individuals to improve and enhance their abilities in order to continue their growth and development over time.

Inspiration and Serving as an Example:

Mentors and coaches play the function of role models, encouraging those under their tutelage to model their positive characteristics, work ethic, and beliefs after their own and directing them toward making choices and decisions that are inspired by their experiences.

The Role of Mentors and Coaches in a Variety of Situations and Contexts:

Academics and Continuing Education for Professional Purposes:

Mentors and coaches offer individuals in academic and professional contexts advise on career pathways, the development of skills, and networking opportunities, so assisting individuals in making informed decisions and achieving success in the domains in which they have chosen to work.

Competition in Sports and Athletics:

Mentors offer emotional support and assistance to athletes, helping them negotiate the demands of competitive sports. Coaches play a critical role in training athletes, perfecting their talents, and strategizing for competitions. In sports and athletics, coaches play a crucial part in training athletes.

Business and entrepreneurial endeavors:

Mentors in business and entrepreneurship provide aspiring business owners with helpful insights, advice, and opportunity to network, thereby assisting the aspiring business owner in navigating the hurdles of beginning and expanding a profitable business.

Growth and development on a personal level:

Mentors and coaches play an important role in the process of personal growth and development by offering advice on topics such as self-improvement, goal planning, and overcoming personal problems. This helps to cultivate a sense of self-awareness and empowerment.

Mentors and coaches who are successful will employ the following strategies and methods:

Listening with attention and empathy:

Effective mentors and coaches engage in practices such as active listening and empathy. This allows them to comprehend the points of view and worries of their mentees and offer support and direction that is founded on mutual respect and recognition.

Defining one's objectives and setting one's expectations:

Fostering a feeling of direction and purpose may be accomplished by mentors and coaches through the establishment of clear goals and expectations for their mentees. This helps mentors and coaches match their guidance and support with the particular needs and ambitions of their mentees.

Providing Feedback That Is Constructive :

By helping mentees recognize areas in which they could grow and improve through the delivery of constructive criticism in a manner that is both encouraging and supportive, mentors can cultivate an environment that values lifelong education and progression.

Creating an Environment That Promotes Autonomy and Independence:

Encouragement of autonomy and independence gives mentees the power to take ownership of their own growth, to make decisions based on accurate information, and to cultivate the self-confidence and resiliency necessary to prevail over obstacles and failures.

Creating an Atmosphere That Is Uplifting and Encouragement-Focused:

The development of a sense of trust and camaraderie between mentors, coaches, and mentees can be facilitated by cultivating an environment that is upbeat and encouraging. This, in turn, can promote open communication, teamwork, and mutual respect.

Encouragement of a "Growth Mindset"

A culture of resilience and perseverance is fostered when mentors encourage their mentees to embrace challenges, learn from setbacks, and regard hurdles as opportunities for learning and development. This is accomplished through the promotion of a growth mindset.

Offering Resources in the Form of Mentorship and Coaching:

Additional assistance and direction can be provided to mentees by providing access to resources, tools, and educational materials that are pertinent to the mentees' areas of interest or requirements for development. This makes it possible to have a mentoring or coaching experience that is full and well-rounded.

Testimonies and Examples of Past Achievements:

In the sport of basketball, Coach Phil Jackson:

Phil Jackson is famous for his accomplishments as a coach in the NBA. He is celebrated for his ability to mentor players not just in their physical skills but also in their personal growth and leadership development. As a result, his teams have won a number of championships, and his players have undergone significant personal improvement.

In the realm of business leadership, Indra Nooyi is an excellent mentor:

PepsiCo's former Chief Executive Officer, Indra Nooyi, has been lauded for her position as a mentor and guide, notably for the way she supports and encourages women in leadership roles. As a result, a great number of people have been motivated to follow their professional goals and strive for excellence.

The coaching achievements of Sir Alex Ferguson in soccer:

It is well known that Sir Alex Ferguson, the famed former manager of Manchester United, had a successful coaching career and was a mentor to many young soccer players. As a result of his guidance, many of these players went on to achieve tremendous success in their careers, both on and off the field.

4.4 Inspirational stories of individuals benefiting from cricket

Cricket is more than simply a sport; it has the potential to change lives, motivate individuals to achieve greatness, and cultivate a feeling of community. Through the years, the sport of cricket has provided peace, a purpose, and a path to success for a large number of people who come from a variety of settings and experiences. During this investigation into uplifting anecdotes, we will learn how the sport of cricket has been a driving force behind individual development, the overcoming of challenges, and the improvement of communities.

1. **Breaking Down Obstacles Presented by Gender Mithali Raj:**

   Mithali Raj, a pioneering personality who broke down gender barriers in the sport of cricket during her time as captain of the Indian women's cricket team, is an example for others to follow. Mithali encountered several obstacles throughout her life, including societal expectations that conflicted with her desire to pursue a career in cricket. She was born in a tiny hamlet in India. Despite this, she never gave up and went on to become one of the most successful and well-known cricket players in the history of women's cricket. Her life serves as a powerful illustration of the transformative potential of dedication and enthusiasm, and she has encouraged other young women to pursue their ambitions in the sport of cricket.

2. **Malala Yousafzai: A Shining Example of the Power of Hope**

   During her time as a refugee in Birmingham, United Kingdom, after escaping a Taliban attack in Pakistan, Malala Yousafzai, the recipient of the Nobel Peace Prize and an advocate for girls' education, found solace in the sport of cricket. She threw herself into the sport of cricket as a means of assimilating into her new community and recovering from the trauma she had endured. Not only did Malala discover her own inner strength through the sport of cricket, but she also made friends and became a symbol of hope for many people all across the world. Her experience exemplifies both the restorative potential of physical activity and the tenacity of the human spirit.

3. **James Anderson: Conquering Obstacles and Difficulties**

   Throughout his career, England's best wicket-taker in Test cricket, James Anderson, had to overcome a number of obstacles, including injuries and other types of setbacks. However, thanks to his dogged persistence, tireless work ethic, and undying passion for cricket, he was able to triumph over these challenges and establish himself as one of the game's most accomplished fast bowlers. His life serves as an example to aspiring cricketers, demonstrating that with hard work and determination, one can do great things. His story is an inspiration.

4. **Rashid Khan, a Shining Example of Hope for the People of Afghanistan**

   The Afghan cricketer Rashid Khan, who is renowned for his remarkable bowling talents, hails from a country that has been afflicted by conflict and instability for a long time. The people of Afghanistan have gained hope and pride as a result of his meteoric journey to popularity on the world cricket stage. The narrative of Rashid exemplifies the potential of cricket to bring people together since it has served as a source of motivation and happiness for a nation that is working toward peace and recognition on the international scene.

5. **Redefining Fielding, According to Jonty Rhodes**

   Jonty Rhodes, a former cricketer from South Africa, is credited with revolutionizing the fielding strategy used in cricket. He established a new benchmark for the level of athleticism and agility required on the field, thereby serving as a model for cricket players of the future.

   His career serves as a model for younger players, encouraging them to rethink their fielding skills and improve their overall contribution to the club.

6. **Virender Sehwag: From Desperate Circumstances to Stardom and Beyond**

   Virender Sehwag, a former Indian cricketer who is best remembered for his aggressive approach to the game, was born and raised in a relatively unimportant village in India. He came from a poor family but eventually became a famous cricket player on an international level. Because of his tremendous journey, we are reminded that everyone, regardless of where they come from or what they've been through, has the potential to achieve extraordinary success if they have talent and put in the effort.

7. **Henry Olonga, a Spokesman for the Cause of Justice**
   During the 2003 Cricket World Cup, the former Zimbabwean cricketer Henry Olonga took advantage of his platform to speak out against the violations of human rights that were taking place in his home country. His brave act of protest, which included donning a black armband to mourn the "death of democracy" in Zimbabwe, was an inspiration to many people and brought attention to the injustices that the people of his nation endure on a daily basis. The story of Olonga exemplifies the ability that sports have to influence culture and bring about positive transformation.

8. **Ellyse Perry, an Outstanding Performer in Multiple Sports**
   Ellyse Perry, an Australian athlete who competes in both cricket and soccer, exemplifies what it means to be successful in a variety of sports. Her adaptability, hard work, and talent in both cricket and soccer have motivated younger players to follow their interests in a wide variety of sports. The lesson to be learned from Perry's narrative is how important it is to celebrate one's unique set of skills and passions.

9. **Ravichandran Ashwin, an Advocate for Educational Excellence**
   Ravichandran Ashwin, an Indian cricketer, is well-known not just for his ability to bowl with spin but also for his support of educational causes. He is of the opinion that education is a potent instrument for the development and liberation of the individual. The fact that Ashwin is so dedicated to both his studies and his cricket career exemplifies the importance of a well-rounded education and the possibility for athletes to serve as advocates for various educational initiatives.

10. **Wheelchair Cricket Champions: Pushing the Boundaries of Their Sport**

Wheelchair cricket champions like Pakistan's Javed Choudhary and Nepal's Paras Khadka have shown that one's physical restrictions do not have to prevent them from having a passion for the game of cricket. They have defied all odds in order to participate at the top levels, demonstrating the force of dedication and the appeal that the sport has across the board.

These uplifting accounts shed light on the myriad ways in which the sport of cricket has made a significant contribution to the lives of countless people. Cricket has been an instrument of emancipation, joy, and inspiration for both players and fans in a variety of ways, including the shattering of gender barriers and the provision of hope in times of tragedy. These anecdotes serve to remind us of the life-altering potential of sports, including cricket, which has the ability to transcend boundaries and affect people's lives in profound ways. They are a shining example of the indomitable human spirit and the power of cricket to bring together, motivate, and elevate people of all different backgrounds and walks of life.

Chapter 5

Playing Cricket for All Ages

Cricket is a sport that appeals to people of all ages since it provides entertainment, positive effects on one's health, and opportunities for participation in one's community. The appeal of cricket will always be there, whether it's for young children learning how to use a bat and ball for the first time or for seasoned veterans savoring the subtleties of the sport. In the course of this in-depth investigation, we dig into the significance of playing cricket at various times of life, the benefits it brings to players on both a physical and mental level, and the ways in which it helps communities feel more united.

A Guide to Cricket for Children (Ages 5 to 12):

1. **Fitness and Coordination in Physical Activity:**
   Children who participate in cricket can benefit from increased hand-eye coordination, physical fitness, and agility. The fact that fielding, batting, and bowling all involve diverse sets of actions makes baseball a well-rounded activity for the general physical development of its players.

2. **Acquiring Important Life Skills:**
   Kids that play cricket develop important life skills like teamwork, discipline, and patience. They learn how to gracefully handle both success and disappointment as well as how to interact successfully with their peers as a result of this.

3. **Increasing One's Self-Confidence:**
   Children's improved levels of confidence and feelings of competence come as a direct result of their achievements in cricket. It inspires them to visualize what they want to accomplish and motivates them to work toward that end.

4. **Interaction with Other People:**
   Because cricket is a team activity, it provides children with the opportunity to engage in conversation with their contemporaries, acquire the skill of cooperation, and establish long-lasting friendships.

5. **Having a Good Time and Enjoyment:**

Most importantly, children will enjoy playing cricket. A excellent incentive to keep oneself physically active and maintain a healthy lifestyle is the thrill of scoring a boundary run or taking a wicket.

A Guide to the Game of Cricket for Adolescents and Teens (Ages 13 to 19):

1. **The Acquisition of Skills:**
   When adolescents reach their teenage years, they begin to focus more intently on improving their cricketing abilities and methods. They can focus on a particular aspect of the game, such as batting, bowling, or fielding, and they typically receive more expert instruction.

2. **Condition of the Physical Body:**
   Teenagers who play cricket are more likely to retain a healthy level of physical fitness. They stay physically active and in good condition by consistently playing in matches and doing regular practices.

3. **Relaxation Techniques:**
   Teenagers often struggle to find a healthy balance between the demands of their academic and social lives. They can reduce tension, retain focus, and have a good balance in their lives by playing cricket, which provides them with a healthy outlet.

4. **Developing One's Character**
   The sport of cricket instills in adolescents the values of perseverance, patience, and the significance of sportsmanship. It contributes to their development as unique individuals and instills ideals that they can take with them into adulthood.

5. **Relationships with Others:**

During their formative years, adolescents frequently develop deep connections with their teammates, thereby establishing a support network that can prove to be of great use.

Young Adults between the ages of 20 and 35 can play cricket here.

1. **Possibilities for Competitive Advantage:**
   Young people frequently take part in local and regional leagues, club cricket, or college cricket, all of which offer them opportunities to compete and show off their skills.

2. **The state of one's health and fitness physically:**
   Keeping active in cricket is an excellent way to maintain both one's physical fitness and one's general health. It's a fantastic opportunity to be active and lower the chance of developing health problems due to sedentary lifestyle choices.

3. **Methods for Coping with Stress:**
   The pressures that come from work and other aspects of life can be difficult. Cricket offers a means of relieving tension as well as recharging one's batteries.
4. **Community and Professional Networking:**
   Young adults often feel a sense of community in the cricketing communities in which they participate. They create useful networks and contribute to a feeling of belonging in the community.
5. **Possibilities for a Professional Career:**

Cricket offers a number of potential professions for young adults, including that of player, coach, and administrator. Beyond just playing the game, there are several professional opportunities available in cricket.

Adults (ages 36 to 60) can play cricket here

1. **Physical Conditioning and the Upkeep of One's Health:**
   Adults can continue to benefit from playing cricket as a means to improve their overall physical fitness and better manage their health. It aids with weight management and has benefits for the cardiovascular system.
2. **Relationships with Others:**
   Many individuals find their social lives enriched by participating in cricket leagues and clubs. They are able to form friendships with people who share similar interests because of this opportunity.
3. **Striking a Balance Between Work and Home Life:**
   Cricket is a sport that helps offer a sense of equilibrium between one's professional and personal lives. It provides relief from the pressures and duties of daily life.
4. **Perfection of Abilities:**
   The complexities of cricket are typically easier for adults to grasp than they are for children. They have the opportunity to hone their skills and serve as a role model for younger athletes.
5. **A Feeling of Satisfaction and Achievement:**

Gaining a sense of success and reinforcing one's interest for a game can be accomplished by reaching certain milestones, such as obtaining a high score or a haul of five wickets.

Cricket for Seniors (Players Must Be 61 or Older):

1. **Interaction with Other People:**
   Cricket is a terrific activity for senior citizens to participate in since it keeps them socially engaged. It gives one the feeling of being a part of a community and of belonging.

2. **Engaging in Physical Activity**
   Cricket enables seniors to enjoy the benefits of physical activity without placing an undue amount of pressure on their bodies, which is essential for maintaining good health in older adults.

3. **Activities that stimulate the mind:**
   Cricket, which requires players to strategize and make decisions, is beneficial for seniors because it stimulates their minds and gives them a sense of purpose.

4. **The Transmission of Know-How:**
   Senior players frequently act as mentors to younger players, passing on their knowledge and expertise, which is extremely beneficial for the continuation of the sport.

5. **A Devotion for a Lifetime:**

Cricket has been a lifelong interest for a lot of elderly people. Their happiness and sense of accomplishment come from being able to play the sport that they adore.

The Numerous Positive Effects That Playing Cricket Can Have On Your Body At Any Age:

Cricket is a great sport to play if you want to improve your cardiovascular fitness because it requires a lot of running. It encourages a healthy heart and good blood circulation throughout the body.

Weight Management: Maintaining an active lifestyle through cricket assists in weight management and helps prevent obesity, which is a risk factor for a variety of health problems.

Health of the Bones Playing cricket requires weight-bearing motions, which are good for bone health and reduce the incidence of osteoporosis and fractures.

Mental Health Cricket provides benefits to mental health in the form of reduced stress, increased opportunities for social engagement, and a heightened sense of achievement.

Coordination and Flexibility: The sport of cricket involves a high level of flexibility, coordination, and reflexes, all of which contribute to an increase in overall physical fitness.

The following are some of the cognitive advantages of playing cricket at any age:

Participating in a team sport such as cricket is an excellent method to release tension and unwind from the demands of everyday life.

Cricket is a sport that needs quick decision-making, strategic thinking, and adaptation, all of which contribute to an increase in mental agility.

Endorphins are chemicals that are produced in the body during exercise. These endorphins have been shown to improve mood and lower the risk of depression.

Interpersonal Communication: Cricket encourages the formation of social relationships and offers a support structure, both of which serve to lessen feelings of loneliness.

In cricket, a sense of purpose and fulfillment can be cultivated through the process of goal setting and accomplishing those goals.

Cricket's Contribution to the Development of Community:

Cricket is played all over the world, bringing people together from all sorts of different cultural and ethnic backgrounds. This helps to promote cultural understanding and exchange.

Participation in Local Communities Cricket clubs and teams frequently participate in their local communities by arranging activities such as events, coaching sessions, and charitable endeavors.

Cricket clubs play a big role in the cultivation of young potential by providing a structured environment for the development of skills and personal growth. Youth Development Cricket clubs play a significant part in the cultivation of young talent.

Cricket matches and tournaments are generally considered to be communal activities because of their ability to bring people together and give them a sense of belonging.

Cricket players, particularly those that compete at a professional level, are frequently looked up to by members of the community as potential role models and sources of inspiration.

Enjoyment, improved health, and participation in one's community are just few of the benefits that come with a lifetime of cricket play. The value of the sport's mental and physical benefits cannot be overstated, while the ability it possesses to construct and fortify communities is beyond limit. Cricket is a sport that creates a shared passion for the game and brings together people of all ages, from young children learning the fundamentals to senior citizens appreciating the complexities of the game. It is a monument to cricket's enduring allure and the universal significance it holds in each of our lives.

5.1 Cricket as a youth sport

The lives of young players are profoundly influenced by cricket, a sport that is popular all over the world due to its long and illustrious history. Cricket is a popular activity among young people because it provides numerous advantages, including the promotion of physical and mental growth as well as the development of social abilities and collaboration. This in-depth investigation dives at the relevance of cricket in the lives of young people, its role in molding personality and self-control, as well as the tactics and efforts that contribute to its rise as a youth sport.

Comprehension of the Significance of Cricket as a Sport for Young People:

Developing Necessary Competences:

Young players can learn valuable skills, such as hand-eye coordination, agility, and strategic thinking, by playing the sport of cricket. These abilities serve as a basis for overall growth in both the physical and cognitive domains.

Developing Collaborative Capabilities and Teamwork:

Young players are taught the value of teamwork and collective accomplishment through the sport of cricket, which is played in a team context and emphasizes collaboration, communication, and friendship among its participants.

Fostering Discipline and Concentration:

Because young players are required to consistently train, adhere to the rules, and be able to concentrate when playing matches, cricket is an excellent sport for instilling discipline and focus in its participants.

Developing a Keen Interest in Physical Activity:

Young players are encouraged to adopt fitness as a basic component of their general well-being as a result of the cricket's physical demands, which in turn promote an active lifestyle among this demographic.

The Promotion of Good Sportsmanship and Fair Play:

Young players learn to respect their opponents, umpires, and the overall ethos of the game through the sport of cricket, which places a strong emphasis on the need of good sportsmanship and fair play.

The Importance of Cricket in the Formation of Young Minds:

Growth in terms of the body:

Young players' motor skills, endurance, and flexibility can all benefit by playing cricket, which makes a positive contribution to their total physical development. It helps address the issues that come with youth engaging in sedentary behavior and encourages a healthy lifestyle overall.

Stimulation of the Mind:

Participating in cricket helps boost cognitive growth because players learn to strategize, assess game circumstances, and make split-second decisions, all of which improves their mental agility and their capacity for critical thinking.

Wellness in Emotional Aspects:

Young players can use cricket as an outlet to manage stress, improve resilience, and maintain

their emotional well-being by playing the sport. Their entire morale is improved as a result of the increased sense of accomplishment and self-confidence that it develops.

Integration into Society:

Young players' sense of belonging and ability to integrate into society is aided by the development of their social skills, the formation of lasting ties with their teammates, coaches, and classmates, and the formation of friendships through the game of cricket.

Formation of Character :

Young players that participate in cricket have their personalities significantly influenced by the sport, which helps inculcate in them important life lessons such as tenacity, integrity, modesty, and leadership—skills that are necessary for both personal and professional development.

Initiatives and Strategies to Increase Participation in Cricket Among Young People

Programs for the Development of Young People:

Establish youth development programs that offer young cricket fans opportunity for thorough coaching, skill development, and mentoring, with the goal of igniting their enthusiasm for the sport at a young age and fostering their interest in it from an early age on.

Programs for the Integration of Schools:

Students will have access to structured training and competitive venues if you collaborate with educational institutions to make cricket a part of the school curriculum or extracurricular activities.

Activities for Participation in the Community:

Organize community-based cricket events, workshops, and competitions that aim to promote community engagement, encourage youth participation, and highlight the beneficial influence that the sport has on young players.

Modules of Instruction That Include Everyone:

Create training modules that are all-inclusive and adapt to the varied requirements and capabilities of young players. This will ensure that all young players have equal opportunity for participation and the development of their skills, regardless of their background or previous experience.

Programs to Promote Coaching Excellence:

Implement coaching excellence programs that place an emphasis on the training and certification of coaches so that they can effectively mentor and assist young athletes.

These programs should also highlight the significance of using constructive coaching tactics and mentorship.

The Development of Infrastructure:

Make investments in the development of cricket infrastructure, such as well-maintained grounds, training facilities, and equipment, in order to offer young players with an atmosphere that is suitable for learning and practicing the sport.

Initiatives Towards Gender Equality:

Encourage gender equality in cricket by facilitating the active engagement of young girls in the sport through the implementation of initiatives such as specific coaching programs, competitions, and other activities that create an atmosphere that is friendly and welcoming to everyone.

The Integration of Technology:

It is important to take use of technological advances in cricket training, including as video analysis, virtual coaching tools, and performance monitoring systems, in order to improve the overall quality of the learning experience and the development of young players' skills.

Programs for Mentoring Young People:

Establish youth mentorship programs that link young players with experienced cricketers or coaches. This will provide the young players with the direction, support, and inspiration they need to continue pursuing their passion for cricket and achieving their goals.

Cricketers who have achieved success and who serve as an inspiration to younger players:

The Indian cricketer Sachin Tendulkar:

The journey of Sachin Tendulkar, widely regarded as one of the best cricketers of all time, began when he was a little boy. This exemplifies the transforming potential of early exposure to cricket as well as the impact it may have on the formation of a legendary career.

Originally from Australia, Ellyse Perry:

Ellyse Perry's extraordinary successes in cricket at a young age have motivated countless females to continue their enthusiasm for the sport. This highlights the need of fostering gender equality and inclusivity in junior cricket programs. [Cricket] is a sport that can be played by everyone, regardless of gender or sexual orientation.

(From Pakistan): Babar Azam:

The meteoric rise to fame of Babar Azam as a gifted young cricketer is illustrative of the relevance of giving extensive opportunities for youth development and cultivating an environment that is supportive of the development of cricketing talent from an early age.

New Zealand's very own Sophie Devine:

The value of comprehensive training programs for young players that emphasize the development of skills, sportsmanship, and character is shown by Sophie Devine's achievements both in youth cricket and at the international level. These programs should place a priority on skill development, sportsmanship, and character development.

The Indian athlete Prithvi Shaw:

The early success that Prithvi Shaw has had in cricket is a tribute to the significance that structured youth development programs play, as well as the impact that committed coaching and mentoring have on the development of the potential of young cricket players.

5.2 The importance of cricket for adults

Cricket, a sport that is typically linked with both amateur and professional competition, is also of significant importance to adults. Many people use it as a way to keep their bodies active, cultivate social ties, and protect their mental health. We dig into the relevance of cricket in the lives of adults, as well as its function in fostering physical fitness, its impact on social ties, and the good benefits it has on mental health, as part of this in-depth investigation.

Wellness and the Maintenance of a Healthy Body:

Fitness of the Cardiovascular System:

Running, sprinting, and fielding are all fantastic forms of cardiovascular training; cricket incorporates all three of these types of movement. These exercises speed up the heart rate, promote blood circulation, and contribute to general improvements in cardiovascular health.

Physical toughness and mental fortitude:

Strength and stamina are essential for the sports of batting, fielding, and bowling. Adults who play cricket on a regular basis are better able to grow and maintain their muscular strength and endurance, both of which contribute to their overall physical well-being.

Management of One's Weight:

Cricket is a sport that requires physical exercise, which is beneficial for managing weight and shedding excess pounds. It is beneficial to both the burning of calories and the maintenance of a healthy body weight.

Ability to Adapt and Move Easily:

The motions involved in cricket, such as fielding and batting, require a high level of flexibility and agility. These characteristics of the game are beneficial to the health of joints and lower the danger of becoming injured.

Stimulation of the Mind:

Cricket's strategic elements, such as game planning, decision-making, and focus, give mental stimulation, allowing people to remain cognitively active and interested during the game.

Connectivity to others and a sense of community:

Friendship and cooperation:

The sport of cricket is frequently played in a team setting. The sense of community and belonging that comes from being a member of a cricket team makes it possible for adults to form enduring connections with the other players on their squad.

Participation in the Community:

Cricket is played all across the world, and many communities have teams and clubs dedicated to the sport. They frequently organize events, competitions, and coaching sessions, all of which encourage participation from and interaction within the community.

The importance of diversity and inclusion:

Cricket is a sport played all around the world and brings together people from all kinds of different backgrounds. As a result, it fosters a sense of inclusiveness and fosters cultural interchange, as it brings together players from a wide variety of nationalities.

Relationships within the Family and Across Generations:

Cricket is a sport that people of all ages may participate in and enjoy to varying degrees. It makes it possible for grownups to form stronger bonds with their children and other members of the family around a common interest in playing the game.

Regional Happenings:

Matches and tournaments of cricket, whether they take place in neighborhood parks or at the level of a club, can draw large crowds and foster a feeling of community by bringing together individuals who share a passion for the sport.

Psychological health and general well-being:

Relaxation Techniques:

Participating in stress-relieving activities such as cricket can be quite beneficial. Individuals are better able to relax and feel less stressed as a result of the game's requirements of both physical exercise and mental attention.

Positive Affect Modification:

Endorphins, which are the body's natural mood boosters, are released when you engage in physical exercise. One's mood can be improved, symptoms of depression can be lessened, and one's general level of happiness can grow by playing cricket.

Confidence in oneself:

Whether it be by scoring runs, taking wickets, or contributing to the team, being successful at cricket gives one a feeling of satisfaction and boosts one's self-confidence.

Being Present and Maintaining Concentration:

Players in cricket must maintain a high level of attention and awareness in order to successfully focus on the current game circumstances, devise appropriate strategies, and execute their plans. These features improve one's mental clarity and overall presence.

Adaptability and Managing Stress:

Cricket teaches adults resiliency through its many obstacles, both positive and negative. They gain the valuable ability to manage with disappointments and setbacks, which is a necessary talent in life.

The Importance of Cricket in the Life of an Adult:

Adulthood and the Pursuit of Physical Activity:

When we are adults, our professional and personal duties frequently take precedence over our desire to engage in physical activity. Cricket is a fun approach to combat sedentary behavior and maintain an active lifestyle, both of which can contribute to a variety of health problems.

Maintenance of a Healthy Work-Life Balance:

The pressures that come from both one's professional and personal lives can be overpowering at times. Adults can find a method to satisfy their demand for amusement and relaxation while still maintaining a healthy balance of their obligations by playing cricket.

Developing One's Personality and Core Values:

Cricket continues to play an important part in the development of character, imparting virtues such as tenacity, integrity, modesty, and leadership in its players. Adults can gain in their personal and professional life from adhering to these ideals.

A Source of Happiness:

For adults, playing a game of cricket can bring both excitement and a sense of accomplishment. Contributing to one's enjoyment and sense of well-being include experiences such as the rush of scoring runs, the satisfaction of taking wickets, or simply enjoying the game itself.

The Roles of Mentoring and Leadership:

Adults frequently serve as mentors and team leaders, directing younger players and passing on

their knowledge, expertise, and experience. This role has the potential to be satisfying and can give a sense of purpose.

Adult cricketers who have achieved success and served as an inspiration:

The Australian, Ryan Harris, says:

Despite suffering from a number of ailments throughout his career, the Australian fast bowler Ryan Harris had a spectacular playing career. Adults who continue to participate in the sport they love can take encouragement from his commitment to the game and his tenacity in the face of adversity.

Defending champion Shivnarine Chanderpaul of the West Indies:

The West Indian cricketer Shivnarine Chanderpaul enjoyed a lengthy and fruitful career in the sport. His longevity and consistency are examples of the importance of effort and passion in the game of cricket for grownups.

Matthew Hoggard, from the United Kingdom:

English fast bowler Matthew Hoggard had a successful second half of his career and was an important cog in England's historic Ashes victory in 2005. Hoggard's success came late in his career. His experience demonstrates that a person is never too old to realize their ambitions in the sport of cricket.

In the words of Lisa Sthalekar (Australia):

After taking some time off from playing cricket, former Australian women's cricketer Lisa Sthalekar was able to make a successful comeback to the sport. Her story serves as a good example of how adults may still be successful in the sport of cricket.

Members of a Cricket Club:

There are countless club cricketers all around the world who play the game simply because they love it. These individuals act as role models for grownups. They are evidence of the evergreen attraction of cricket as a pastime and a means of achieving one's potential.

5.3 Promoting active aging through cricket

Active aging is a philosophy that encourages people of retirement age to lead meaningful lives by being mentally, physically, and socially involved throughout their later years. Cricket, which is typically thought of as a sport for younger people, has recently been acknowledged as a way for older people to promote active aging in themselves. We dive into the relevance of cricket in the lives of seniors, including its role in improving physical health, maintaining mental acuity, and cultivating social relationships during the golden years of life in this in-depth investigation.

Advantages to One's Physical Health:

Fitness of the Cardiovascular System:

Running between the wickets in cricket is a great way to improve your cardio-vascular fitness because it works all major muscle groups. It aids in the preservation of a healthy heart and circulatory system in elderly people.

Both Solidity and Equilibrium:

In the sport of cricket, batting, bowling, and fielding all demand a certain level of muscular strength and balance. Participating in these activities makes a positive contribution to one's overall physical health.

Wellness of the Joints:

The movements of cricket help to enhance joint flexibility and mobility, which can relieve typical age-related ailments such as stiffness and arthritis.

Management of One's Weight:

Cricket is a sport that requires players to engage in physical activity, which helps players maintain a healthy weight and prevents obesity, which is a risk factor for a variety of health problems.

Health of the Bones:

Cricket is a sport that features weight-bearing movements, which are good for bone health and lower the risk of osteoporosis and fractures.

Sharpness of mind and good cognitive health:

Stimulation of the Mind:

Due to the strategic nature of cricket, players must be able to make snap decisions, focus intently, and evaluate situations critically. The mental stimulation provided by these activities is beneficial to the cognitive health and mental agility of senior citizens.

Methods of Solving Problems:

Players in cricket are required to strategize, adjust to changing circumstances, and make judgments while they are competing on the field. This helps elders develop their problem-solving skills while also keeping their minds active and stimulated.

Improvements to One's Memory:

Memory and recall skills can be improved by the demands placed on cricket players, such as the requirement to remember game plans, previous performances, and the relative strengths and weaknesses of opponents.

Relaxation Techniques:

Seniors can effectively handle stress and anxiety by participating in cricket, which is good for their mental health and promotes overall well-being.

Lifting of Spirits:

Endorphins, which are the body's natural mood boosters, are released when you engage in physical exercise. Seniors who participate in cricket have a lower chance of developing depression and a better overall mood.

Participation in Social Life and Connection to One's Community:

The company of another:

Companions and a sense of belonging are two benefits that come hand in hand with being a part of a cricket team, regardless of whether or not you play in official leagues. This is of utmost importance for senior citizens who run the risk of being socially isolated.

Bonds that span multiple generations:

People of all ages and stages of life frequently come together to watch cricket. It is possible for seniors to create meaningful intergenerational relationships with younger players through bonding activities.

Activities for the Community:

Matches and tournaments of cricket are frequently held as community events, as they attract people and help foster a sense of community. It is possible for seniors to take an active role in and engage with the community around them.

Mentorship is defined as:

Senior cricket players have the ability to act as guides for newer players, imparting the vital knowledge and expertise that they have gained over their careers. This helps ensure the longevity of the sport.

Examples to Follow:

Senior cricketers who continue to compete in the sport are an inspiration to younger athletes because they show that age does not have to be a limiting factor when it comes to pursuing one's interests.

Increasing Physical Activity in Older Adults Through Cricket Initiatives:

Programming for Walking Cricket:

Walking cricket is a version of cricket that has been adapted so that it may be played by older people. Several organizations now provide walking cricket programs. With this style, senior citizens are able to keep active at their own pace while still enjoying the activity.

Cricket Leagues for Recreational Purposes:

Leisure cricket leagues and clubs cater particularly to senior citizens, providing a laid-back and pleasurable setting in which elderly citizens can take part in the sport of cricket.

Workshops for Instructional Purposes:

Seniors can become more familiar with the sport of cricket by participating in instructional workshops and sessions that focus on the game's rules, techniques, and history.

Tournaments Open to the Public:

It is possible to create a chance for senior citizens to get together and celebrate the sport of cricket by organizing community competitions in which senior citizens are encouraged to participate.

Assistance with Mental Health:

The incorporation of mental health support services into cricket programs for elderly citizens can assist in addressing the emotional and psychological elements of aging, hence assuring complete well-being for the participants.

Ability to Participate and Accessibility:

It is essential for the advancement of active aging to ensure that cricket facilities are accessible to older people, regardless of their level of mobility, and to develop an inclusive environment within the sport.

Stories of Triumph and Inspiring Performances by Senior Cricketers:

Wilfred Rhodes (from the United Kingdom):

The fact that Wilfred Rhodes continued to play cricket in his 52nd year is a tribute to the everlasting passion that elderly citizens have for the game of cricket and the opportunities that exist for active aging through the sport.

Grace Appleton, who hails from Australia:

Grace Appleton, an Australian cricketer, kept playing club cricket well into her 70s. Her career spanned several decades. Seniors find motivation in her unwavering commitment and infectious energy.

Groups Who Play Cricket While Walking:

Numerous walking cricket organizations all around the world have proved the beneficial effects of modified formats that make the sport accessible to older folks and promote active aging. This has led to an increase in the number of elderly people participating in the sport.

Activities for the Community:

Local cricket communities that actively include elders in matches and events have proven that the sport is a powerful instrument for building social connections and active aging. [Cricket] communities have shown that the sport is a powerful tool for developing social connections and active aging.

Teams Comprised of People of Different Ages

Teams that feature a mix of senior and younger players bring attention to the sport's amicable coexistence of players of varying ages, highlighting the important role that cricket plays in the development of intergenerational connections.

5.4 Overcoming barriers and stereotypes

Cricket, like many other sports, has had its fair share of obstacles to overcome, including prejudices and restrictions, which have hampered the sport's ability to be inclusive and equitable. We look into the problems that have traditionally plagued cricket, the preconceptions that have limited participation, and the efforts that have been taken to break down these barriers, fostering a more inclusive and equal playing field for all. This in-depth investigation is presented here.

The Obstacles of the Past:

Colonial Inheritance :

Because of its roots in British colonialism, many people have the impression that cricket is an elite and closed-off sport. Because it was brought to many countries through the process of colonialism, people have a tendency to think of cricket as a game played by the upper class.

Disparities in the Economy:

A substantial obstacle might be presented by the high expense of cricket equipment and facilities. Many aspiring players, particularly those who come from economically disadvantaged families, may not have access to appropriate equipment or training facilities.

Discrimination Based on Gender:

Throughout its entire existence, cricket has been played almost exclusively by men. It was difficult for women to participate in cricket due to the lack of available opportunities and resources, which contributed to the perpetuation of gender gaps in the sport.

Discrimination Based on Race:

In some areas, racial prejudice has created an environment that is hostile to players of certain racial or ethnic backgrounds, which has led to discrimination against those players. As a consequence of this, many exceptionally bright people have been denied equitable access to opportunities.

Cricket has its fair share of cliches:

"Gentlemen's Game" :

The perception that cricket is a "gentlemen's game" has contributed to the spread of the misconception that it is a sport that is only played by those of high social standing. The sport is now divided along class lines as a result of this stereotype.

"Men's Game" :

Many women have been dissuaded from pursuing cricket due to the widespread belief that the sport is played exclusively by men, which has resulted in less opportunities for female cricket players.

"Slower Pace" :

The perception that cricket moves at a slower pace than other sports has contributed to widespread misunderstandings regarding the sport's level of physical demand and enthusiasm.

"Traditionalist Sport" :

The general public's conception of cricket as an archaic and resistant to change sport has, at times, acted as a barrier to the development of new strategies and techniques inside the game.

Activities Conducted in an Attempt to Foster Inclusivity and Equality:

Initiatives Towards Gender Equality:

Significant strides have been made toward gender equality in cricket thanks to initiatives such as the inclusion of women's cricket in major tournaments, equal pay for female players, and programs to encourage girls to join in the sport.

Programs for the Development of Young People:

Scholarships, free coaching programs, and access to cricket facilities are examples of initiatives that can assist alleviate economic inequities. Other examples include programs that target the development of young talent from disadvantaged areas.

Policies that Seek to Eliminate Discrimination:

The governing bodies of cricket have instituted anti-discrimination regulations and have taken a resolute stand against racism and other types of prejudice.

Programs for Promoting Diversity and Inclusion:

Individuals from a wide variety of backgrounds are encouraged to take part in the sport of cricket by organizations and clubs that promote diversity and inclusion within their ranks.

Bringing the Game Up to Date:

Cricket has been made more accessible to a wider audience as a result of innovations such as T20 cricket, which emphasizes shorter formats and more dynamic play. This has made the sport more thrilling.

Some Examples of Successful Overcoming of Obstacles and Typecasting:

Team Afghanistan of the Cricket:

The Afghanistan national cricket team has competed successfully on the international level despite coming from a land that has been ripped apart by conflict. Their voyage has disproved many preconceived notions about the exclusive nature of cricket.

The Era of Anti-Apartheid Struggle in South Africa:

The struggle that South Africa waged against apartheid in the sport of cricket ultimately resulted in the elimination of racial segregation in the game, which helped to advance inclusiveness and equality.

The Indian Women's Cricket Team:

A nation that is obsessed with cricket saw its attitudes on women's cricket shift as a direct result of the Indian women's cricket team's success, particularly in the ICC Women's World Cup in 2017.

The Improvement of Ireland in Cricket:

The lightning-fast ascent that Ireland has taken in cricket, including the attainment of Test status, exemplifies how drive and effort can break down barriers, regardless of the country's previous experience with cricket.

People Challenging Their Own Preconceived Ideas:

The success of a large number of cricketers who came from disadvantaged upbringings, such as M.S. Dhoni in India, demonstrates that talent and devotion can triumph over preconceived notions regarding one's socio-economic status.

The Path That Lies Ahead:

Educational Programs and Activities:

Education about the inclusiveness, history, and principles of the sport of cricket can help dispel stereotypes, and it can be promoted in schools and by cricket organizations.

Increasing Participation in Grassroots Cricket:

It is essential to break down barriers by fostering grassroots cricket at the community level, with a focus on diversity and equitable opportunity.

Programming for Mentoring:

The development of mentorship programs, in which more experienced cricket players coach younger players, can assist individuals in overcoming preconceptions and navigating obstacles.

Representation in the Media:

Helping to dismantle harmful notions about cricket can be accomplished through responsible media coverage and positive portrayals of players who come from a variety of backgrounds.

The importance of inclusivity in leadership:

It is possible for cricket organizations to produce more inclusive policies and decisions if they encourage diversity in leadership roles within the company.

The progression of cricket toward inclusiveness and equality has been highlighted by the sport's successful navigation of historical obstacles and the shattering of prejudices that have hampered the involvement of specific communities. The landscape of cricket has become more diversified and welcoming as a result of efforts to eliminate discrimination, support youth who come from disadvantaged backgrounds, and promote gender equality. Cricket is a sport that can be played by anybody, regardless of their background or identity, and the stories of people and teams who have overcome these hurdles and found success serve as both an inspiration and a reminder of this fact. As cricket continues to develop and embrace openness and equality, it becomes a beacon of hope for overcoming prejudices and discrimination in the wider world of sports and society. This is because cricket is an inclusive and equitable sport.

Chapter 6

Cricket and Mental Health

Cricket, a sport that is frequently lauded for the strenuous physical requirements and intricate strategic complexities it entails, also plays a crucial part in players' mental health and overall well-being. In this in-depth investigation, we dive into the complex relationship between cricket and mental health. We discuss the difficulties that cricket players have to deal with, the impact that the sport has on their psychological well-being, and the steps that are being made to promote mental health within the cricket community. This inquiry digs into the mental aspects of cricket, covering topics such as the demands of competition and the significance of seeking help when necessary.

Comprehending the Mental Demands Placed on Cricket Players:

The Spiral of Performance Pressure:

Players are put under a significant amount of pressure to maintain consistent performance at all levels of cricket, but especially at the professional level. In the game of cricket, those who bat are expected to score runs, bowlers must try to take wickets, and fielders must perform flawlessly in the field.

Managing Setbacks and Defeats:

Failure is an integral aspect of the game of cricket, which is why it's such a popular sport. Batsmen are frequently dismissed for having poor scores, while bowlers are sometimes put through difficult stints. It is a huge difficulty to be able to deal with the emotional toll that can be taken by one's failures.

Ailment and Rehabilitation:

Cricket players frequently have injuries, and the subsequent long road to rehabilitation can be mentally demanding. It can be difficult to find a balance between the irritation of being unable to play and the anxiousness of getting back into the game after a break.

Protracted Departures and Isolation:

Cricketers who compete on the international stage frequently spend extended amounts of time away from home, which can contribute to feelings of alienation and homesickness. The extended periods of time spent alone can be taxing on a person's mental health.

The Examination of the Media and the Views of the Public:

Cricket players who play professionally are subjected to continual media scrutiny, and public opinion can be critical. The emotional toll that can be taken from having to contend with criticism, personal assaults, and unreasonable expectations can be significant.

The Effect on a Person's Mental Health

Anxiety, as well as Stress:

Cricket players might experience significant levels of anxiety and stress as a result of the pressure to perform well and the dread of falling short of expectations. During competition, anxiety can make it difficult to make decisions and maintain attention on the task at hand.

Depression and Physical Exhaustion:

The monotony of playing cricket, combined with the stress placed on performers, can lead to feelings of despair and exhaustion. Players have a chance of getting dejected and worn out when playing this game.

Regard for oneself and sense of self-worth:

A player's self-esteem and sense of self-worth, as well as their confidence on and off the field, might suffer when they have a string of setbacks.

Isolation and a Feeling of Being Alone:

Because service members are often away from their families and friends while on tours, they

may experience feelings of isolation and loneliness, which can have a negative effect on their mental health.

Concerns Regarding One's Body Image and Eating Disorders:

The constant focus on a player's physique and level of fitness can be a contributing factor in the development of eating disorders and issues with body image, especially among younger cricket players.

Taking the Following Steps to Improve Cricket Players' Mental Health:

Teams that Provide Support for Mental Health:

A wide variety of cricket boards and organizations have begun establishing mental health support teams, which often consist of psychologists and counselors. These trained specialists offer aid and therapy to players who are struggling with issues related to their mental health.

Education of the Players:

In order to raise awareness about the significance of mental well-being and to decrease stigma, educational programs on mental health are incorporated into player development.

Participant Organizations:

Player associations work to preserve the rights and well-being of players, including campaigning for assistance and services related to mental health. In doing so, player groups promote the rights of players.

A Time of Rest and Relaxation:

For the sake of the players' mental health, it is imperative that the off-season be structured in a way that allows for sufficient time for rest and recovery.

Conversations That Are Open:

Cricket players are strongly encouraged to have honest discussions about mental health and to share the experiences they've had. This contributes to the reduction of stigma and normalizes the act of seeking help.

Examples of Victories in the Fight for Mental Health Advocacy:

The Australian scientist Glenn Maxwell:

In 2019, Glenn Maxwell decided to step away from cricket in order to concentrate on his mental health. Because he was so honest about his issues, many other cricket players have made mental health a priority in their careers.

Sarah Taylor, from the United Kingdom:

Sarah Taylor, a well-respected English cricketer, has been open and honest about her struggles with anxiety and the significance of getting professional assistance when necessary.

(Speaking for South Africa) Shaun Pollock:

Former South African captain Shaun Pollock has spoken publicly about his struggles with depression and how reaching out for assistance from trained professionals made a big impact in his life.

Author James Faulkner from Australia says:

James Faulkner has discussed his struggles with anxiety and how he overcame them with the help of treatment and support from friends and family.

The Englishman Marcus Trescothick says:

Marcus Trescothick's open and honest depiction of his battles with depression and anxiety has been an important factor in the cricket community's progress toward removing the stigma that surrounds mental health.

The following are resources and strategies for mental health:

Support from Professionals It is essential to handle difficulties relating to mental health by seeking assistance from professionals in the field of mental health, such as psychologists and counselors.

Meditation and Mindfulness: Techniques such as meditation and mindfulness can assist cricket players in better managing stress and anxiety, enhancing their ability to focus, and generally improving their mental health.

Communication and Support Systems The establishment of robust communication and support systems within teams enables players to discuss their issues and obtain support from their teammates.

Strategies for Managing Stress Learning strategies for managing stress, such as time management, goal setting, and relaxation exercises, can assist players in coping better with the effects of pressure.

Maintaining a Balanced Lifestyle It is essential for one's mental health to keep a balanced lifestyle, which includes making time for one's family, hobbies, and relaxation.

The Path That Lies Ahead:

Continued Advocacy It is crucial for those involved in cricket to continue their efforts to promote mental health awareness and support. It is an ongoing process to encourage open conversations and break down stigmas that surround issues pertaining to mental health.

Information: Making sure that young cricketers have information on mental health from the very beginning of their careers might be helpful in preventing and resolving concerns later on in their careers.

Support for Retired Players It is extremely important to offer retired cricket players who may have difficulty making the transition away from professional cricket support in the areas of mental health.

Fostering a Holistic Approach to Player Development It is essential, for the purpose of generating well-rounded and resilient cricket players, to foster a holistic approach to player development that takes into account mental, emotional, and social components.

Inclusivity and Diversity: Addressing issues of discrimination and bullying, in addition to encouraging inclusivity and diversity in cricket, can help to improve the mental well-being of all participants.

6.1 Cricket as a therapeutic tool

Cricket, a sport that is revered for the spirit of competition and the physical demands it places on its participants, also has the potential to be used as a therapeutic tool. Beyond the confines of the cricket field, the sport has the potential to develop a sense of community while also fostering both physical and mental well-being in its participants. In this extensive investigation, we dig into the myriad of ways in which cricket can function as a therapeutic tool, benefiting people as well as communities.

Wellness and the Treatment of Physical Disabilities:

Cricket is a fantastic activity for achieving and maintaining a healthy level of physical fitness. Running, sprinting, bowling, and batting are all components of the sport, all of which offer participants the opportunity to increase their cardiovascular fitness, strength, and agility.

Cricket can be used as part of rehabilitation programs for those who are healing from injuries, and this can be a beneficial use of the sport. The healing process can be helped along by returning to the sport in a manner that is both managed and gradual.

Weight Management: Taking part in cricket on a regular basis can help with weight management and weight loss, both of which contribute to improved overall physical well-being.

Joint Mobility: The motions involved in cricket, such as fielding and batting, help to increase joint mobility and flexibility. As a result, the risk of stiffness and injuries is decreased.

Endorphins are the body's natural stress relievers, and when you engage in physical exercise like playing cricket, your body will release endorphins, which can improve your mood and help you feel less stressed.

Psychological health and general well-being:

Reducing Stress: Playing cricket is a great way to take your mind off of stressful situations and give yourself a chance to unwind. The level of concentration and focus that is necessary in the game might serve as a welcome distraction from the stresses of everyday life.

Enhancing one's mood through physical activity, such as the sport of cricket, can lift one's spirits and lessen the intensity of depressive symptoms. The sense of camaraderie and accomplishment that comes from participating in the sport both contribute to an increased mental well-being.

Awareness and focus: The tactical aspects of cricket need awareness and focus, which in turn improves mental sharpness and presence.

Cricket teaches players how to deal with challenges, disappointments, and setbacks, which instills perseverance and vital life skills. Players can learn these abilities through playing the game.

Cricket is a team sport, so participating in it with other people can help cultivate a sense of belonging and provide an opportunity for social interaction, both of which are essential to maintaining mental health.

Formation of Communities and Strengthening of Social Ties:

Participation from the Community Cricket clubs and organizations frequently host events, competitions, and coaching sessions in order to promote participation from and interaction within the local community.

Cricket is a worldwide sport that brings together persons from a wide range of backgrounds for the purpose of cultural exchange. As a result, it fosters a sense of inclusiveness and fosters cultural interchange, as it brings together players from a wide variety of nationalities.

Cricket matches and tournaments, whether they take place in local parks or at the club level, frequently draw audiences and help to establish a feeling of community by bringing together people who share a passion for the sport.

Cricket is a sport that can be enjoyed by people of many ages, making it a great option for building intergenerational and family bonds. It makes it possible for grown-ups to form stronger bonds with their children and other members of the family around a common interest in playing the game.

Cricket community programs and events bring people together, which helps to establish social links and foster a sense of belonging. These are the types of activities that fall under the category of "local initiatives."

Developing One's Personality and Core Values:
Individuals gain the valuable life skills of perseverance and resilience as a result of the obstacles and ups and downs that they experience while playing cricket. These are abilities that can be applied in a variety of contexts.

Leadership and Responsibility: Within a cricket team, leadership positions are frequently need to be filled. Participants gain the ability to assume responsibility and make choices that have an impact on the result of the game.

Teamwork: Because playing cricket requires cooperation and teamwork, it teaches its participants the importance of pulling together to achieve a common objective.

Fair Play Cricket is a sport that places a strong emphasis on sportsmanship and fair play, with the goal of encouraging players to behave in an honest and ethical manner both on and off the field.

Self-discipline: The level of dedication needed to be successful at cricket instills a level of self-discipline that may be applied to many different facets of one's life.

Transformational Stories Full of Motivation and Inspiration:
Street Cricket in India: Organizations in India have been effective in using cricket as a means to engage impoverished youngsters and give them with a road out of poverty and a brighter future through the usage of the sport.

Individuals who have a physical disability have been given the opportunity to demonstrate their skills and talents through the sport of disability cricket. This has enabled these individuals to break down societal barriers and alter people's perceptions of them.

Women's Cricket: The achievements and expansion of women's cricket have disproved preconceived notions about gender roles and encouraged young girls and women to follow their athletic goals.

Cricket programs in prisons have proven to be an excellent method for rehabilitating offenders, teaching them essential life skills, and lowering the rate of recidivism.

Community Cricket Leagues Community cricket leagues at the local level have helped to unite people of varying backgrounds and establish communities that are resilient and supportive of one another.

Ways to Increase Awareness of Cricket as a Potential Treatment Method:
Community Initiatives: In order to encourage social interaction and engagement, community cricket activities, competitions, and coaching sessions should be organized.

Educational Outreach Cricket can be included into the educational programs of schools and other groups, allowing for the teaching of important life lessons as well as the benefits of teamwork and physical activity.

Assistance for Mental Health Integrate services for mental health assistance into cricket programs in order to address the emotional and psychological facets of well-being.

The cultivation of youthful talent, the provision of scholarships, and the facilitation of access to cricket facilities should be the primary focuses of youth development efforts.

Inclusivity and Diversity: Ensure that persons from a wide variety of backgrounds, regardless of socioeconomic level, gender, or physical ability, are able to participate in the sport of cricket.

The Obstacles to Overcome and the Way Forward:

Cricket has made achievements in promoting inclusivity, but there is still work to be done to ensure that the sport is accessible and welcome to everyone, regardless of their background or identity. Inclusion While cricket has made strides in promoting inclusivity, there is still work to be done.

Mental Health Despite the growing recognition of the importance of the topic, the mental health side of cricket still requires ongoing attention, including efforts to increase awareness and decrease stigma.

Cricket has an enormous potential to strengthen communities and foster social links, but this potential has not yet been fully used to its fullest. This is especially true in areas of the world where cricket is not as widely played.

Education and Development It is essential for the growth of young cricketers to ensure that they receive a well-rounded education that addresses not only their intellectual but also their emotional and social needs.

Continued Advocacy It is vital for the wider awareness and impact of cricket as a therapeutic instrument, including both physical and mental well-being as well as community building. Continued advocacy for cricket as a therapeutic tool.

6.2 Personal growth and self-esteem

The general health and happiness of an individual, as well as their level of achievement in life, are inextricably linked to their level of personal development and self-esteem. They are connected in the sense that a person's level of self-esteem has a substantial impact on the path they choose toward personal development, and that personal development, in turn, can help raise self-esteem. In this essay, we will investigate the complex link that exists between personal development and self-esteem. We will look at the significance of these concepts on their own, as well as the ways in which they complement and strengthen one another.

1. **The Crucial Role of Self-Esteem in the Process of Personal Development**
   Personal development cannot occur without first establishing a strong sense of one's own self-esteem, also known as a person's self-worth or regard for oneself. It is a reflection of an individual's entire assessment of their value as a person, taking into account their abilities, qualities, and worth. People who have a healthy sense of self-esteem are more likely to be open to the idea of personal growth and development because they have faith in their ability to grow, learn, and adjust to new circumstances.

The Importance of Self-Esteem in Motivation

Individuals' levels of self-esteem are a significant factor in the degree to which they are motivated to work on improving themselves. People who have a healthy sense of their own worth are more likely to strive for lofty goals, be willing to take calculated risks, and be resilient in the face of adversity. They have faith in their own potential and have faith in their ability to overcome challenges; this motivates their quest for personal improvement. They believe in their ability to conquer challenges.

The Role of Self-Esteem in Developing Resilience

A robust feeling of self-worth acts as a buffer against the negative effects of failure and setbacks. People who have a strong sense of their own worth are more resilient and better able to recover quickly from the setbacks that are inevitable in life. This sort of resilience is an essential component of individual development because it helps people to draw wisdom from their past experiences and to continue advancing in their lives.

2. **The Continual Path Towards Individual Development**

   The journey of self-improvement, learning, and development that constitutes personal growth is one that continues throughout a person's entire life. It covers many elements of a person's life, such as their intellectual, emotional, social, and physical development, among others. The pursuit of personal growth is motivated by the desire for self-fulfillment as well as a more in-depth understanding of one's capabilities.

   Establishing and Accomplishing One's Objectives

   The process of goal-setting and -accomplishment is frequently the starting point for personal development. These objectives can be professional, personal, academic, or even connected to one's passions and interests outside of work. As individuals strive toward achieving these goals, they are consistently increasing their knowledge and abilities, which, in turn, enhances their sense of self-worth.

   Learning Without Stopping

   A dedication to one's own ongoing education is one of the most important components of personal development. This requires the acquisition of new information, capabilities, and experiences. Learning helps people become more adaptable, open to change, and confident in their capacity to manage new problems, all of which contribute to a rise in self-esteem. Learning also helps people become more receptive to new experiences.

3. **The Relationship Between Individual Progress and Sense of Self-Worth**

   The relationship between an individual's personal development and their sense of self-worth is one that is two-way and mutually supportive. Improvements in an individual's self-esteem are one of the side effects of engaging in the process of personal growth. A greater level of self-esteem, on the other hand, is necessary for the development of the motivation and resiliency necessary for personal growth.

Self-Esteem is Enhanced by One's Own Personal Growth

Stepping outside of one's comfort zone, taking on new challenges, and attaining success in various facets of one's life are common components of the process of personal growth. These accomplishments provide a favorable contribution to an individual's overall sense of self-esteem. The individual's self-esteem is bolstered to the extent that they are successful in overcoming challenges, acquiring new abilities, and accomplishing their objectives, so establishing a positive feedback loop.

Personal development is driven by healthy self-esteem.

On the other hand, self-esteem serves as a driving force behind personal development. When people have faith in themselves and their capabilities, they are more likely to accept opportunities for personal development and take calculated risks. People with higher self-esteem are more likely to challenge themselves, seek out new experiences, and take the required actions to promote their own personal development.

4. **Methods for Promoting Healthy Self-Esteem and Continuing Personal Development**

Reflection on Oneself and Acceptance of Oneself

To get started, think about the things you've accomplished in the past as well as your strong and weak points. Acknowledge that you are not perfect and work on accepting yourself as you are. Realize that blunders and setbacks are a natural and expected part of the process, and that they can provide invaluable learning opportunities.

Establishing Objectives and Making Plans

Create a list of measurable, attainable, and relevant goals that are in line with your personal development objectives. Separate each of these objectives into a series of more doable actions. This strategy gives you the ability to monitor your development and recognize your accomplishments at various points along the journey, which is beneficial to your sense of personal pride.

Learning Without Stopping

Accept the challenge of learning new things and improving yourself throughout your entire life. Continuously extending your knowledge and abilities, whether through formal education, self-study, or hands-on experiences, will not only assist you in achieving your personal development goals but will also increase your sense of self-worth.

Try to Get Some Help and Opinions.

Participate in a support group consisting of people such as friends, family, mentors, or therapists who are able to offer encouragement and critical comments. Their insights have the potential to assist you in recognizing both your strengths and areas in which you may make improvements, thus bolstering your sense of self-worth.

Personal development and healthy self-esteem are inextricably linked and mutually supportive of one another. Self-esteem naturally rises alongside a one's pursuit of personal development; conversely, a higher sense of one's own value as a person inspires that individual to continue working toward personal development. Both of these things are necessary for leading a life that is successful and satisfying. Individuals are able to unlock their full potential, become more resilient, and acquire a sense of empowerment that opens the way for a brighter and more rewarding future if they grasp the mechanics of this relationship and actively nurture both personal growth and self-esteem.

6.3 Stories of individuals using cricket to overcome mental health challenges

Cricket, which is commonly referred to as the "gentleman's game," possesses a special power that can bring people together regardless of their background or culture. Cricket is not just a well-known sport, but it has also served as a wellspring of motivation for those who are struggling with issues related to their mental health. In this essay, we will look into the lives of various individuals who have turned to cricket as a means of coping with, and ultimately overcoming, their mental health concerns. Specifically, we will focus on how these individuals overcame their conditions as a result of their involvement in cricket. These anecdotes shed light on the therapeutic characteristics of the game as well as its capacity to build resiliency, give a sense of purpose, and boost general mental health and wellness.

1. **The Rehabilitative Effects of Crickets**

   A Medium for Establishing Connections

   Cricket is more than simply a sport; it's also a community-building pastime that brings people together. Cricket fosters a sense of community and belonging among its players, regardless of whether they are engaging in a friendly game in the park or competing in a league setting. This feeling of being connected is really helpful for persons who are battling challenges with their mental health. It makes it possible for people to interact with one another, so minimizing feelings of isolation and building supportive relationships.

   Both mental and physical well-being benefit from exercise

   It is well established that taking part in physically demanding pursuits like playing cricket can have a beneficial effect on one's mental health. Endorphins, which are natural mood boosters, are the chemicals that are released when you exercise. The sport of cricket, which requires players to run, bat, and field, is an excellent way to enhance one's physical fitness while also lowering one's levels of stress, anxiety, and depression.

2. **Success and Victory Narratives**

   The Long and Winding Road Out of Depression That Sam Took to Become Team Captain

   After a string of defeats in his personal life, Sam, a young man who was passionate about cricket, found himself struggling with despair. The weight of his disability, coupled with feelings of loneliness and self-doubt, made living day-to-day a struggle for him. On the other hand, a fortuitous meeting with a local cricket team completely altered the course of his life.

Sam decided to join the group in order to get out of his shell and rediscover a sense of direction in his life. Cricket ended up becoming his salvation, as it provided him with a routine and a purpose to get out of bed each morning. His self-esteem and confidence grew as he worked to better his talents and developed relationships with the other members of his team. In only a few short years, Sam moved from being a novice who was having trouble getting by to becoming the team captain. This position provided him with a fantastic feeling of accomplishment and purpose. His involvement in cricket not only led to an improvement in his mental health but also motivated him to assist others who find themselves in a situation analogous to his own.

The Struggle That Emma Faces with Her Anxiety and Low Self-Esteem

Cricket was first shown to Emma, a young woman who had a history of anxiousness as well as low self-esteem, by a friend who had the hope that the sport could assist Emma in overcoming the issues that she was facing. Emma's initial reaction was one of reluctance due to the fact that she had never shown any interest in participating in athletics and she was concerned about the opinions of others.

She was taken aback by the warmth and welcome she received from the cricket community. Her friends supported her efforts to develop her skills and broaden her perspective, encouraging her to strive for progress rather than perfection. Emma's uneasiness eventually subsided as she became more self-assured in both her on-field and off-field endeavors. She was able to confront her insecurities within the protected setting of the cricket team, and the activity served as a channel for her to physically release the feelings that were building up inside of her. The experience of Emma highlights the efficacy of cricket in enhancing one's sense of self-worth and reducing feelings of worry.

3. Cricket as a Means of Relieving Stress and Anxiety

Adam's Story of Overcoming Adversity and Trauma

Post-traumatic stress disorder (PTSD) is something that Adam, a veteran of the military, struggles with because he was exposed to horrible events while he was serving. The constant nightmares, flashbacks, and heightened awareness made living day to day feel like an impossible task. Adam's results from traditional therapy were not very encouraging, so he was eager to find an alternative.

Adam's introduction to cricket came about when he joined a support group for veterans. The activity helped him channel the pent-up energy he'd been carrying around and diverted his attention away from the horrific memories he'd been reliving. A reassuring feeling of structure was provided by the fact that the requisite discipline in cricket was quite similar to the discipline he had learned in the military.

Adam was able to restore a sense of control and confidence as a result of his involvement in cricket throughout the course of time. It allowed him to communicate with other veterans who had been through similar experiences and introduced him to a community that was supportive and understanding. For Adam, playing cricket evolved into a therapeutic outlet that helped him manage his post-traumatic stress disorder and rebuild his life.

The Steps That Led Barry Back to God After His Time in Rehab

Barry's life had become consumed by addiction, which led to his losing his work, his family, and his sense of what he was worth as a person. The bottom of the barrel appeared to be his only reality until he found out about a cricket program that was designed to assist those who were recovering from addiction.

The structure, collaboration, and discipline of the sport gave Barry with the support he required to begin the process of rebuilding his life. He replaced his bad habits with a passion for the game of cricket, which eventually became his new addiction. Barry's self-esteem improved as he worked hard to perfect his abilities, and he found comfort in the companionship of his teammates, many of whom had been through difficult times themselves. Barry was able to turn his life around with the assistance of cricket, earning the trust of his family and discovering a revitalized sense of purpose in the process.

4. **Initiatives in the Community to Improve Mental Health, Primarily via Cricket**

Programs for Cricket on the Street

Street cricket initiatives have emerged as a beacon of light for disadvantaged children and teenagers living in difficult environments in a number of different urban places. These programs offer young people a secure and welcoming setting in which they can gain valuable life skills, improve their sense of self-worth, and direct their energy in a constructive direction. Cricket serves as the medium via which individuals interact with role models and peers, which in turn promotes personal development and mental toughness.

Cricket Adapted for Players of All Abilities

The objective of the "Cricket for All Abilities" movement is to broaden access to the sport of cricket for people with a variety of impairments, including intellectual and physical impairments. These programs make it possible for people of varying abilities to take part in the activity, and they frequently place more of an emphasis on the social aspects and the development of skills than on actual competition. The participants in these programs can potentially experience significant improvements in their mental health as a direct result of the increased sense of belonging and accomplishment that they acquire from participating in these programs.

5. Obstacles and Things to Take Into Account

Although cricket has been demonstrated to be an effective instrument for the enhancement of mental health, it is crucial to recognize that it is not guaranteed to be a solution that works for everyone. There are some people out there who either have no interest in sports or who find cricket to be intimidating. In addition, the fact that athletic competition is inherent to the sport might, for some people, make performance anxiety or feelings of inadequacy worse.

As a result of this, it is essential for support networks, mental health experts, and cricket organizations to collaborate in order to guarantee that individuals have a variety of choices available to them in terms of receiving assistance for their mental health. Cricket should be seen as one tool among many others in a bigger toolkit for the purpose of alleviating issues related to mental health.

The stories of those who have used cricket as a means of overcoming issues related to their mental health illustrate the capacity of the sport to make positive changes in people's lives. Cricket provides participants with a sense of belonging, physical activity, organization, and social support, all of which can play an important role in the improvement of mental health. Cricket has been shown to be an effective therapeutic outlet for individuals struggling with issues such as low self-esteem, recovery from traumatic experiences, and addiction.

People from all walks of life, regardless of their skills or origins, should be able to experience the therapeutic benefits of cricket because community programs that promote mental health via cricket play a critical part in broadening access to the sport. This ensures that people may benefit from the game regardless of who they are.

Cricket's ability to heal stretches well beyond the bounds of the pitch, bringing hope and a sense of purpose to those who need it the most. As we reflect on these stories of triumph and resilience, it becomes apparent that cricket's power to heal reaches far beyond the boundaries of the pitch.

6.4 Strategies for creating a mentally healthy cricket environment

Communication that is both open and honest is essential to the development of a psychologically sound cricket environment. All members of the organization, including players, coaches, and support staff, should feel at ease when expressing any issues, struggles, or triumphs related to their mental health. The stigma that is associated with mental health can be broken down via conversation, making it simpler for individuals to seek assistance when it is required.

Programs to Raise Awareness of Mental Health

It's possible that running programs to raise awareness about mental health in cricket clubs, schools, and teams might be quite helpful. Participants in these programs can be educated about prevalent mental health concerns, warning signals, and options that are available to them. Individuals are better able to detect those around them who may be struggling and provide help for them if there is increased awareness.

Access to the Support of Professionals

Every cricket club and organization should have an easy means to get in touch with mental health professionals, such as counselors and psychologists, if they feel the need. When a player needs assistance or sees a fellow teammate in need, they should know who to turn to for help and where to find it. Giving players access to specialists who are familiar with the specific demands that come with playing cricket can make a major difference.

Networks of Peers Who Help Peers

The development of peer support networks within of cricket teams or clubs can prove to be extremely beneficial. A great amount of support can be obtained from having colleagues who are able to empathize with one another's situations and who are willing to provide an ear when needed. These networks have the potential to be proactive in the promotion of mental well-being by arranging workshops, group discussions, and activities for groups that are centered on mental health.

Instruction on the Management of Stress

The sport of cricket puts its players in high-pressure circumstances on a regular basis, which can cause stress and anxiety. The ability to adequately cope with these stresses can be facilitated in players through the education of stress management techniques such as deep breathing, visualization, and mindfulness. The ability to spot the warning signs of stress and offer sound advice on how to deal with it should be part of a coach's standard training.

Foster a healthy balance between work and life

Cricket players frequently have to balance several commitments, such as employment or school, with their training and their participation in tournaments. It is crucial to encourage a healthy work-life balance in people. The time that players spend on their personal lives should be respected, and players should be given enough time to relax and recuperate. It is possible to avoid burnout and other problems with mental health by making one's well-being a higher priority than excessive training.

Establishing Objectives That Can Be Met

One of the most important things that can be done to foster a mentally healthy environment in cricket is to set goals that are attainable and realistic. The players and the coaches should work together to devise objectives that will test the players while yet being within their capabilities. Having expectations that cannot be met will almost certainly result in frustration and will have a detrimental influence on one's mental health.

Activities that Strengthen the Bonds Within a Team

Participating in activities designed to foster team togetherness and a sense of belonging can be beneficial to a cricket team. These activities help establish trust and support among teammates, which contributes to an environment that is more positive and welcoming to everyone. When players have a strong sense of connection to their team, they are more inclined to discuss their mental health concerns and seek assistance when necessary.

Get rid of the stigma

One of the primary goals is to eliminate the shame that is associated with mental health problems. Players, coaches, and administrators should all make concerted efforts to foster an environment in which requesting assistance for issues related to mental health is not stigmatized as a sign of lack of strength. Encourage the idea that taking care of one's mental health demonstrates both strength and the ability to bounce back from adversity.

Encourage people to take care of themselves

In order to maintain a mentally healthy atmosphere, it is vital to place an emphasis on self-care. It is important that players are encouraged to take care of their mental and physical well-being by engaging in activities such as getting a sufficient amount of sleep, keeping a balanced diet, and practicing relaxation techniques. When it comes to emphasizing the significance of self-care and implementing it themselves, coaches may set a good example for their athletes.

Assess and keep an eye on your mental health

It is necessary to conduct routine mental health screenings and keep track of the athletes' progress. Changes in an athlete's behavior, performance, or attitude could be an indication of a problem with their mental health; therefore, it is important for support staff and coaches to be attentive and aware of these changes. Early intervention is often essential in order to forestall the development of more serious issues.

Leadership that Includes Everyone

The leaders of the cricket community, including coaches and administrators, should demonstrate what it means to lead in a way that is inclusive. They need to do everything in their power to foster an environment of respect, equality, and support. Within the context of cricket, inclusivity ensures that players of various ages, ethnicities, and experiences can enjoy a sense of belonging while also being protected.

Chapter 7

Female Empowerment through Cricket

The historically male-dominated sport of cricket has recently emerged as a potent instrument for the advancement of women's rights. Over the course of its history, women's cricket has made considerable strides toward its goal of achieving worldwide recognition, respect, and support. This essay analyzes the numerous ways in which female empowerment is being achieved through the sport of cricket, including overcoming gender stereotypes, promoting leadership, self-confidence, and resilience in players, and more. We will go into the history of women's cricket, celebrate the successes of female cricketers, and evaluate the influence the sport has on individuals as well as societies. Ultimately, the goal of this discussion is to emphasize the transformative potential of cricket as a vehicle for female empowerment.

1. **The Development of Women's Cricket Within Its Historical Context**
   The participation of women in cricket may be traced back to the 18th century, which is roughly contemporaneous with the early growth of the sport among males. On the other hand, throughout its history, women's soccer has had to contend with a wide variety of obstacles and prejudices.
   Leaders in the Development of Women's Cricket
   The first known instance of women playing cricket took occurred in England in 1745, when two teams of female players battled against one another at a charitable event. The 19th century was a pivotal time for the development of women's cricket, thanks in large part to the efforts of trailblazers such as Lady Wroth, Lilian Bland, and Lady Clarke.
   The Development of Women's Cricket on an International Stage
   In 1934, England and Australia played each other in what is considered to be the first ever women's international cricket match, so establishing the groundwork for the expansion of women's international cricket. Despite this, for a considerable portion of its history, the sport of cricket played by women has gotten a lot less attention and support than the game played by men.

2. **Obstacles and Generalizations**
   Failure to Provide Adequate Investment and Infrastructure
   Throughout its history, men's cricket has gotten significantly more financial support than women's cricket. The women's game struggled to advance due to a lack of available resources, facilities, and opportunity.
   Stereotypes Regarding Both Sexes
   Many people believed that the sport of cricket was too physically demanding for women or that it was in opposition with traditional gender roles; as a result, women's cricket was frequently hampered by these traditional gender preconceptions.

3. **The Women's Cricket Movement and Its Revolutionary Effects**
   Confronting Preconceived Ideas
   Female cricket players have been instrumental in shattering gender roles and expectations in the sport. The feats they have accomplished and the expertise they have displayed on the playing field have disproved long-held beliefs regarding the potential of women in athletics. They have, as a result, encouraged many young women across several generations to follow their passions despite the pressures placed on them by society.
   Motivating Examples to Look Up to
   Female cricket players have emerged as motivational and empowering role models for young women and girls all around the world. Their stories of perseverance, resiliency, and accomplishment provide a powerful message: with effort and dedication, women can overcome difficulties and accomplish what they set out to do.

4. **Women's cricket as a stage for fostering leadership and empowering women**
   Opportunities to Take the Leadership Role
   Leadership opportunities, both on and off the field, have been developed for women through the
   sport of women's cricket. The traditionally male-dominated leadership roles within the sport are being challenged by the presence of women in these traditionally male-dominated positions.
   Coordination and cooperation as a Team
   Players develop a stronger sense of collaboration, cooperation, and mutual support through their participation in cricket. These abilities transpose into the larger context of women's life, giving them the capability to collaborate with one another to overcome obstacles and accomplish shared objectives.

5. **Beyond Athletics: Opportunities for Personal Development and Autonomy**
   Confidence in oneself and a healthy respect for oneself
   Female players who take part in cricket can expect to grow in both self-confidence and self-esteem as a result of their involvement in the sport. They will feel more valuable to themselves and their team as they continue to develop their

abilities and contribute to the overall success of their team. These experiences of emancipation extend much beyond the confines of the cricket field and have an effect on a variety of facets of their lives.

Capacity for Recovery and Mental Toughness

Players are frequently put under a significant amount of pressure and are faced with difficult situations in cricket. Managing these demands builds resiliency and mental toughness, which enables female cricket players to face challenges with confidence and resolve.

Growth on a Personal Level

Discipline, time management, and the ability to create and achieve goals are all abilities that may be gained from playing women's cricket, which helps contribute to overall personal growth. These characteristics are not only essential in the world of athletics, but they are also applicable in other spheres of life, such as education and professional endeavors.

6. **Grassroots Organizations and Educational Institutions**

   Cricket academies for girls play an important part in the development of talent and in providing access to the sport. Grassroots initiatives also play an important role. These programs provide girls with the opportunity to develop their cricketing abilities and passions by providing them with coaching, infrastructure, and a supportive atmosphere.

7. **Accomplishment and Reputation on the Global Stage**

   Achieving Success on the International Scene

   On the world stage, women's cricket has had an incredible amount of success. Both the Women's Cricket World Cup and the ICC Women's T20 World Cup have evolved into extremely difficult and prestigious competitions in recent years. Women's cricket is gaining more and more attention in the athletic world as both the level of competition and the number of fans around the world continue to improve.

   Equal Treatment and Pay Equity

   Significant headway has been achieved in the fight for female cricket players to be paid and treated on par with their male counterparts. There are a number of cricket boards and organizations that are attempting to achieve gender parity in terms of salary, opportunities, and resources.

8. **Obstacles and Proposed Directions for the Future**

Investing and Building Up the Infrastructure

There is still a significant amount of room for development in the area of financial investment in women's cricket, which includes the provision of facilities, coaching, and opportunities. Continuation of investment may assist in maintaining and enhancing the growth of the sport.

Shifting Mental Attitudes

It is an ongoing process to challenge the deeply ingrained gender stereotypes and societal expectations that exist today. Education and awareness efforts are vital to changing perceptions and creating an environment that is more welcoming and supportive of female cricket players.

Increasing Our Impact Around the World

The participation of women in women's cricket has increased dramatically in a number of nations, but additional work is required to broaden the sport's reach and support in places where it is less well-established.

Development from the Ground Up

It is essential to the continuation of women's cricket's success that talent be nurtured and developed at the grass-roots level. The development of future generations of female cricketers can be aided by financial investments in academies, coaching, and easily accessible facilities.

Women's cricket has evolved into a powerful force for female empowerment, defying preconceptions and creating possibilities for leadership, personal growth, and recognition on the international arena. This is because women's cricket provides opportunity for women to compete against other women from across the world. Female cricket players are more than simply athletes; they are also motivational examples to look up to and advocates for social progress.

It is vital to solve difficulties, invest in infrastructure and talent development, and work towards altering social ideas as women's cricket continues to expand and gain pace. By doing so, women's cricket will be able to continue to shatter stereotypes, break down barriers, and enable girls and women to pursue their aspirations and realize their full potential, not only within the world of cricket but also outside of it. The foreseeable future of women's cricket contains the possibility of even more opportunities for empowerment and equality, as well as even greater levels of achievement.

7.1 Breaking gender stereotypes in cricket

Cricket, which has historically been played more by males than by women, has a long history of being associated with deeply ingrained gender stereotypes, which has resulted in less opportunities for women to participate in the sport. However, over the course of the last few decades, women's cricket has undergone a remarkable metamorphosis. As a result, these prejudices have been challenged, and the landscape of the game has been reshaped. In this essay, we will investigate the process of shattering gender stereotypes in cricket by shining light on the historical context, the primary elements leading to this transformation, and the ongoing work that is required to create a cricketing society that is more inclusive and equal.

1. **Traditional Gender Roles in Cricket Throughout Its History**
   The Preponderance of Men in the Sport
   The history of cricket is rife with gender stereotypes that portrayed males as the primary and, in many instances, the only participants in the game. The fact that

men's cricket received more attention, support, and money helped to sustain the idea that cricket was primarily a male preserve.

Assumptions Regarding Capabilities of the Body

Throughout its history, cricket has been seen as a strenuous sport, which has frequently contributed to the misconception that women are unable to compete on an equal level with males when it comes to coping with the challenges that come with playing the game. Because of this notion, opportunities for women to participate in cricket were restricted, and they had less access to resources and facilities.

2. **Changing the Landscape: Important Considerations in Overcoming Gender Stereotypes**

Pioneering Women in the Sport of Cricket

The emergence of brilliant and driven female cricketers who defied societal expectations and played a key role in shattering gender stereotypes had a significant impact in the development of the sport. These women demonstrated their prowess, resolve, and resiliency, demonstrating that cricket is not solely the preserve of men. Belinda Clark, Charlotte Edwards, and Mithali Raj are just a few examples of the players who have gone on to become motivational examples for subsequent generations.

Enhanced Investment and Provision of Assistance

As a result of women's cricket being seen as a legitimate and marketable sport, cricket boards, organizations, and sponsors have expanded their financial investments and support for the sport. Players now have the option to make a living playing cricket thanks to the creation of women's cricket leagues like the Women's Big Bash League (WBBL) and the Kia Super League. These leagues were established in recent years.

Movements Towards Equal Pay

The expectation that female cricket players should be paid and treated equally became a fundamental driving force for the dismantling of gender stereotypes. Movements such as #EqualPayForEqualPlay gained traction, which resulted in a more balanced division of resources, opportunities, and compensation for female cricket players.

Initiatives at the Local Level

Grassroots programs and academies that are specialized to women's cricket have been extremely helpful in fostering the development of talent and expanding participation in the sport. These programs provide girls with the opportunity to enhance their cricketing skills by providing them with instruction, facilities, and a supportive environment.

Achievements on a Global Scale

The status of women's cricket has improved as a result of the sport's achievements on the international scene, such as the Women's Cricket World Cup and the ICC Women's T20 World Cup. Women's cricket is a sport that is deserving of respect and support since it is a competitive and interesting sport, as proven by the high-quality matches that have been played and the rising fan base.

3. **Challenging Preconceived Ideas Within the Industry**

Competence and expertness

Female cricketers have regularly proved their skill and technique, challenging the misconception that women are unable to play cricket at a high level. [Cricket] is a sport that is traditionally played by men. The women's game of cricket has elevated spectacular catches, strong drives, and pinpoint bowling to the level of expectation.

Conditioning the body

The notion that cricket is too strenuous of a sport for female athletes has been disproved by the success of women's teams in the sport. It has been demonstrated that female cricketers are more than capable of meeting the tough physical requirements of the game as a result of the intensive training, conditioning, and fitness routines that they have adopted.

4. **Beyond the Playing Field: Advancing Women's Empowerment in Cricket**

In cricket, challenging preconceived notions about men and women extends well beyond the playing field, creating an atmosphere in which women can assume positions of authority and take part in a variety of facets of the game.

Both coaching and management are included here.

Within the sport of cricket, women can now be found instructing and holding crucial administrative positions. They play an active role in the decision-making processes, which is vital for encouraging gender equity and diversity within the sport they participate in.

Motivating Examples to Look Up to

Young girls and women might look up to the female cricketers who compete on the professional circuit as empowering role models. Their tales of grit, fortitude, and triumph convey an inspiring message: women can do what they set out to do and triumph over the challenges they face.

5. **Obstacles to Overcome and Work That Remains**

Investing and Building Up the Infrastructure

It is critical to make financial investments in women's cricket, including in terms of facilities, coaching, and chances. There is still a significant gap in resources between many countries, and this issue needs to be addressed if we want to see women's cricket continue to make strides forward.

Shifting Mental Attitudes

The constant struggle of challenging deeply ingrained gender norms and the expectations of society is fraught with difficulty. Education and awareness initiatives are important to change ideas and to create an environment that is more welcoming and supportive of female cricket players.

Increasing Our Impact Around the World

Significant advancements in women's cricket have been made in a number of nations, but there is still much work to be done to increase the sport's popularity and participation in regions where it is not as well developed.

Development from the Ground Up

It is essential to the continuation of women's cricket's success that talent be nurtured and developed at the grass-roots level. The development of future generations of female cricketers can be aided by financial investments in academies, coaching, and easily accessible facilities.

Female cricketers have overcome societal expectations and paved the way for future generations by demonstrating tenacity, drive, and ability on their road to overcoming gender stereotypes in the sport of cricket. This journey is a monument to their accomplishments in this regard. A more inclusive and egalitarian cricketing world has been created as a result of the extraordinary success that women's cricket has made. This advancement challenges traditional norms and perceptions.

Despite the fact that we are celebrating the accomplishments of female cricketers, it is imperative that we acknowledge the fact that our work is not yet done. Investment, shifting mindsets, and extending opportunities are crucial to ensuring that women's cricket continues to thrive and serves as an inspiration for all those who strive to break free from gender stereotypes and pursue their ambitions on and off the cricket field. This will ensure that women's cricket continues to serve as a role model for those who aspire to break free from gender preconceptions and pursue their dreams. The foreseeable future of women's cricket contains the possibility of even more opportunities for empowerment and equality, as well as even greater levels of achievement.

7.2 The rise of women's cricket

The rise of women's cricket is a story of perseverance and tenacity, as well as a journey that has been revolutionary and has transformed the world of cricket. For many years, the sport was mostly seen as belonging to men, and female cricket players had fewer opportunities and received less respect than their male counterparts. However, over the course of the last few decades, there has been a tremendous transition, and women's cricket has emerged as a significant force in its own right. In this essay, we will investigate the journey that led to the rise of women's cricket by tracing its historical roots, analyzing major milestones, and highlighting the impact that it had on the game, players, and societies as a whole.

1. **Setting the Scene in Time**
   Beginnings in the Past
   Women first began competing in cricket matches in the 1740s, which places their beginnings in the 18th century. This is the beginning of the history of

women's engagement in cricket. However, the route that women took to establish their position in the world of cricket was one that was slow and fraught with many obstacles.

Lack of Representation and the Persistence of Gender Stereotypes

Throughout its history, cricket has been regarded as a game that can only be played by men, and deeply ingrained gender stereotypes have maintained the idea that women do not possess the necessary physical capabilities to compete at a high level in the sport. Women's cricket has been further neglected as a result of limited possibilities, a lack of investment, and unequal resources.

2. **Important Turning Points in the Development of Women's Cricket**

The Emergence of Women's Cricket Clubs in the U.S.

In England and Australia, the first women's cricket clubs were established in the latter half of the 19th century and the early 20th century respectively. These groups offered a venue for women to compete against one another and hone their talents, so providing the groundwork for the establishment of organized women's cricket.

The Very First International Contest

In 1934, England and Australia played each other in the first ever international women's cricket match. The match was held in England. Due to the fact that it matched the expansion of men's international cricket, this historic event marked a key stride in the development of women's cricket.

The Development of Various Domestic Leagues

The creation of women's domestic cricket competitions like the Women's Big Bash League (WBBL) in Australia and the Kia Super League in England has breathed fresh life into the sport of cricket. These leagues offered female cricketers the chance to compete at a professional level, which was a significant factor in the development of women's cricket.

Competitions held on a global scale

Both the Women's Cricket World Cup, which was first played in 1973, and the ICC Women's T20 World Cup, which was played for the first time in 2009, have become into prestigious and fiercely competitive tournaments. On the international scene, the relevance of women's cricket was highlighted by the high standard of play as well as the expanding fan base.

Movements Towards Equal Pay

The fight for female cricketers to be paid the same as their male counterparts and receive equal treatment gained steam, which resulted in a more equitable division of resources, opportunities, and incomes within the sport.

Motivating Examples to Look Up to

Belinda Clark, Charlotte Edwards, Mithali Raj, Ellyse Perry, and a number of other prominent female cricketers have become as powerful sources of motivation for younger girls and women who aspire to be like them. Their stories of selflessness, tenacity, and triumph have disproved many preconceived notions and paved the road for others who will come after them.

3. **Challenging Typical Attitudes Regarding Gender**

Competence and expertness

The notion that women are unable of competing successfully at a high level in the sport of cricket is being disproved by female cricketers, who have shown extraordinary skill and technique. They have earned a reputation for making amazing catches, driving the ball powerfully, and bowling accurately.

Conditioning the body

The notion that women cannot play cricket because it is considered to be too strenuous physically has been disproved by the female cricketers' dedication to hard training, conditioning, and fitness regimens. They have demonstrated that they are more than capable of satisfying the strenuous physical requirements that the game imposes.

4. **Women's Empowerment in the Sport of Cricket**

Both coaching and management are included here

Within the sport of cricket, women are increasingly actively participating in coaching and holding major administrative posts. They are breaking established gender norms that are associated with leadership roles by making decisions and contributing to the expansion of the sport.

Motivating Examples to Look Up to

Young girls and women might look up to the female cricketers who compete on the professional circuit as empowering role models. Their experiences demonstrate that women can triumph over adversity and accomplish everything they set their minds to, whether it is in the sport of cricket or in any other facet of life.

5. **Obstacles to Overcome and Work That Remains**

Investing and Building Up the Infrastructure

It is critical to make financial investments in women's cricket, including in terms of facilities, coaching, and chances. There is still a significant gap in resources between many countries, and this issue needs to be addressed if we want to see women's cricket continue to make strides forward.

Shifting Mental Attitudes

It is an ongoing process to challenge the deeply embedded gender stereotypes and societal expectations that exist today. Education and awareness efforts are required in order to make the atmosphere in which female cricket players compete more welcoming and encouraging.

Increasing Our Impact Around the World

It is necessary to make an effort to broaden the reach of women's cricket and the support it receives in areas of the world where the sport is less well established. This involves encouraging the growth of the sport at the grassroots level and expanding participation opportunities.

Development from the Ground Up

It is imperative that talent be cultivated at the grassroots level if the emergence of women's cricket is to continue and be sustainable. The development of future generations of female cricketers can be aided by financial investments in academies, coaching, and easily accessible facilities.

The success of women's cricket is a tribute to the commitment, tenacity, and talent of female cricket players, who have defied the expectations of society and paved the way for future generations. A more inclusive and egalitarian cricketing world has been created as a result of the extraordinary success that women's cricket has made. This advancement challenges traditional norms and perceptions.

Despite the fact that we are celebrating the accomplishments of female cricketers, it is imperative that we acknowledge the fact that our work is not yet done. Investment, shifting mindsets, and extending opportunities are crucial to ensuring that women's cricket continues to thrive and serves as an inspiration for all those who strive to break free from gender stereotypes and pursue their ambitions on and off the cricket field. This will ensure that women's cricket continues to serve as a role model for those who aspire to break free from gender preconceptions and pursue their dreams. The foreseeable future of women's cricket contains the possibility of even more opportunities for empowerment and equality, as well as even greater levels of achievement.

7.3 Profiles of inspirational female cricketers

Women's cricket has gone a long way as a result of the devotion, enthusiasm, and perseverance of a number of remarkable female cricketers who have shattered stereotypes and established new benchmarks within the sport. These athletes have not only broken barriers in terms of their performance on the field, but they have also emerged as significant role models, smashing gender preconceptions and encouraging younger generations of young women to pursue their ambitions. In the following paragraphs, we will provide brief biographies of some of the amazing women who have made an unforgettable impression on the world of cricket.

Belinda Clark, who is from Australia

Belinda Clark, an Australian cricketer, is widely recognized as a pioneering figure in the sport of cricket. In 1991, she made her first appearance for her country in an international competition, and she rapidly established herself as a powerful all-rounder. 1997 marked the year that she made history by becoming the first player, male or female, to ever achieve a double century in a One Day International (ODI) match.

The skills of leadership that Clark possessed were also very outstanding. She led the Australian women's cricket team to a number of successes during her time as captain, including two victories at the Women's World Cup (1997 and 2005). She was awarded the rank of Member of the Order of Australia (AM) for her services to cricket in recognition of her significant contributions to the sport.

Clark has not only made a major effect on the field, but he has also done so off of it. In 2011, she became the first female executive in the history of Cricket Australia, further breaking down barriers and boosting the engagement of women in cricket administration.

Charlotte Edwards, who hails from England

Charlotte Edwards, a former captain for the England women's cricket team, is widely regarded as one of the most iconic individuals in the annals of women's cricket history. The adventure of Edwards started when she was young, and in 1996 she made her debut on an international stage. Because of her graceful batting style, strong leadership abilities, and undying dedication to the sport, she rose to prominence in a hurry.

She led England to multiple successes as captain, including the Women's Cricket World Cup in 2009 as well as three Women's Ashes series victories. Among her many accomplishments as captain, she is most proud of these. Edwards was noted for her ability to adapt her game to a variety of forms and was the first female cricketer to score 2,000 runs in T20 Internationals.

Since Edwards' retirement from international cricket in 2016, she has continued to contribute to the sport in the roles of coach, pundit, and ambassador for women's cricket. In these roles, she actively promotes and cultivates the next generation of female cricket players.

Indian captain Mithali Raj

An illustrious figure in the sport of cricket, Mithali Raj is frequently referred to as the "Tendulkar of Indian women's cricket" because of her success in the game. Since making her first appearance for India in an international match in 1999, she has established herself as one of the most successful run scorers in the annals of women's cricket.

One of Raj's many accomplishments is that she was the first woman to score 6,000 runs in one-day internationals. She has distinguished herself as the captain of the Indian women's cricket team, bringing them all the way to the final of the Women's Cricket World Cup in 2005. In the face of intense competition, Raj always maintains her composure and displays an exceptional batting technique.

In 2017, she broke the record by becoming the first female cricketer to play 200 One-Day Internationals. Because of Raj's unwavering commitment to the activity she plays and her dogged pursuit of victory, countless young women in India and elsewhere in the world look up to her as a source of inspiration.

Ellyse Perry, who hails from Australia

Ellyse Perry is an exceptional all-rounder in women's cricket, and she has represented Australia with distinction in both soccer and cricket. At the age of 16, she made her first appearance for the Australian women's cricket team, and she swiftly established herself as one of the most accomplished all-rounders in the world.

The amazing resume of Perry's cricketing career includes the fact that she holds the record for being the youngest Australian to play in an international cricket match. She is well-known for her fast bowling, excellent batting skills, and the ability to excel in both one-day internationals and twenty-over games. Perry has been an essential contributor to Australia's many achievements, including the country's triumphs in the World Cup and the Women's Ashes.

In addition to her skills in cricket, Perry has also competed for Australia on the national level in the sport of soccer. Her successes in a pair of distinct sports have made her an example for younger athletes who have goals of excelling in a variety of competitions and sports.

Stafanie Taylor, who represents the West Indies

Stafanie Taylor is a well-known cricketer from the West Indian island of West Indies. She is renowned for the remarkable talents and leadership she displays on the cricket pitch. In 2008, she made her first appearance with the West Indies women's cricket team, and she rapidly established herself as a strong all-rounder.

The rise of the West Indies women's cricket team may be directly attributed to the performances of Taylor. She led her team to win in the Women's Twenty20 World Cup in 2016, and she has been a reliable performer in both One-Day Internationals and Twenty20 matches. Her achievements have garnered her a number of accolades, including the title of Women's Cricketer of the Year from the International Cricket Council (ICC).

Off the field, Taylor has been an active participant in a number of projects aimed at fostering the growth of women's cricket in the Caribbean and has aggressively encouraged young women to take up the sport. Her commitment to the sport and her enthusiasm for playing it make her an admirable role model for aspiring young female cricket players.

Meg Lanning, who hails from Australia

Meg Lanning is one of the sport's all-time greats despite the fact that she is currently serving as the captain of the Australian women's cricket team. She made her first appearance in 2011, and she rapidly gained a reputation for her aggressive approach to the plate and her ability to score a lot of runs.

Because of her talents as a leader, Lanning has been instrumental in guiding the Australian team to a number of successes, including two World Cup crowns and three Women's Ashes victories. She became the team's youngest captain in its long and illustrious history, and she has successfully continued the Australian women's cricket team's tradition of success.

Her influence is not limited to the results of her individual performances; Lanning's contributions as a leader and an ambassador for the sport have been extremely important to the expansion of women's cricket in Australia and elsewhere in the world.

Jhulan Goswami, who hails from India

Jhulan Goswami, one of the best fast bowlers in women's cricket, is a pioneering figure for the game in India. She was the first Indian to play the sport professionally. She joined the Indian women's cricket squad for the first time in 2002 and rapidly established herself as a formidable bowler after making her debut.

As a result of her extraordinary career, Goswami has taken the most wickets in women's one-day internationals (ODIs), which is a credit to her talent, consistency, and hard ethic. She has a proven track record of success on the world stage and was presented with the Padma Shri, India's fourth-highest civilian award, in recognition of her achievements to the sport of cricket.

As a result of Goswami's accomplishments, young women in India now have the opportunity to make a living playing cricket, which encourages them to have faith in their own capabilities and overcome obstacles.

Sarah Taylor, who hails from England

Sarah Taylor, an English wicketkeeper-batter, is renowned for her outstanding abilities as a wicketkeeper as well as her beautiful batting. 2006 was the year she made her first appearance for the England women's cricket team, and she was instantly recognized for the contributions she made.

Fearlessness, inventive strokeplay, and the capacity to exert influence on the game are hallmarks of Taylor's contribution to the advancement of women's cricket. She has been a key part of England's victories, including those in the Women's Ashes and the ICC Women's T20 World Cup, both of which England has won.

In addition to her performances, Taylor has not been shy about discussing her struggles with anxiety and other issues related to her mental health. Others have been motivated to seek help and support as a result of her willingness to acknowledge these difficulties, which has helped eliminate the stigma that surrounds mental health in cricket.

The biographies of these outstanding female cricketers who have left an indelible impact on the sport are just a small representation of the remarkable women who have contributed significantly to the evolution of cricket. Their anecdotes are a demonstration of their commitment, talent, and enthusiasm for the game of cricket. They have smashed gender preconceptions, inspired generations of young girls, and contributed to the growth of women's cricket globally. Not only have they achieved great success on the field, but they have also inspired generations of young girls.

These cricket players have shown that gender does not play a role in the game of cricket;

rather, cricket is a game that requires skill, drive, and enthusiasm. They demonstrate to aspiring female cricketers that with commitment and effort, it is possible for them to compete at the highest levels of the sport, serving as role models for these athletes. The growth of women's cricket is in large part due to the contributions of these influential personalities, and the legacy they leave behind will continue to inspire and empower future generations.

7.4 Encouraging women and girls to participate

It's not just about producing female athletes when we encourage girls and women to get involved in sports; it's also about fostering health, self-confidence, and leadership, as well as gender equality. Men have traditionally held a dominant position in sports, which has contributed to significant gender gaps in participation rates, resource allocation, and opportunity availability. It is crucial for the overall development of women and girls to provide opportunities for them to participate actively in sporting activities. At the same time, it is necessary to challenge societal standards that maintain inequality. In the following paragraphs, we will discuss the necessity of removing the barriers that prevent women and girls from participating in sports, as well as the tactics that may be used to promote more inclusivity.

1. **The Significance of Girls and Women Participating in Sports**
   Wellness, both Physical and Mental
   The benefits to one's physical and mental health that come from taking part in sports are numerous. Participating in regular physical activity can aid in the prevention of obesity, lower the risk of developing chronic diseases, and enhance one's general health and well-being. In addition, participation in athletics helps develop self-discipline, strategies for dealing with stress, and mental toughness.
   Self-Respect and Confidence in Oneself
   Participating in sports can assist in the development of self-esteem and confidence. Women and girls who take part in athletics are more likely to feel a sense of accomplishment, learn how to create and reach objectives, and cultivate a good image of their bodies. These characteristics are essential to their development as individuals and to their success in a variety of facets of life.
   Leadership and the Empowerment of Others
   Women and girls can strengthen their leadership and collaborative abilities, as well as their resiliency, through participation in sports. Participating in sports gives students the skills necessary to overcome obstacles, figure out solutions, and guide other people, which in turn increases their likelihood of being successful in academics, careers, and other areas of life.
   Equality of the Sexes
   One of the most important things that can be done to advance gender equality is to create more opportunities for women and girls to get involved in sports. It challenges established gender roles, preconceptions, and societal standards that have, historically speaking, hindered the participation of females in a variety of sectors, including sports.

2. **Obstacles Facing Women Who Want to Participate in Sports**
   Customs and mores of both cultures and societies
   The cultural standards of many societies are strongly engrained, and they place an emphasis on the traditional gender roles. As a result of these conventions,

women and girls are frequently discouraged or prevented from participating in athletics because it is commonly believed that such activities are incompatible with femininity.

Inaccessibility and a lack of facilities

One of the most major obstacles can be a lack of proper access to sporting facilities and equipment. It can be challenging for women and girls to take part in sporting activities since in many areas there are insufficient resources and facilities available to support their participation.

Misconceptions and Prejudices

The media and our culture frequently reinforce gender stereotypes, which can be detrimental to the self-esteem of women and girls and discourage them from participating in athletics. The underrepresentation of women in athletics can be attributed, in part, to preconceived notions such as "girls aren't as competitive as boys" and "sports are for men."

Pressure from Peers

Girls may be dissuaded from participating in sports by both the pressure from their peers and the fear of being judged by their peers. The urge to live up to the standards set by society and protect oneself from being teased or laughed at can be a potent dissuader.

A dearth of examples to emulate

Girls may be less motivated to participate in sports if they do not see any female role models doing those sports. When kids do not see other women succeeding in sports, it is more difficult for them to imagine themselves doing well in such arenas.

3. **Methods to Encourage Female Participation in Athletics and Other Sports**

Several different approaches can be used in order to provide a more welcoming environment in sports and to encourage women and girls to take part in athletics.

Encourage Learning and Consciousness-Raising

It is extremely important to raise knowledge about the benefits that come from female participation in sports. Educational initiatives and programs have the potential to combat preconceived notions and biases while also educate communities about the many benefits of participating in sports.

Develop Athletic Settings That Are Open To Everyone

It is important for communities, schools, and sports organizations to work together to actively establish situations that are welcoming to women and girls as well as safe for them to engage. This includes the provision of proper facilities and resources, as well as the establishment of policies that have zero tolerance for discrimination based on a person's gender.

Put an end to preconceived notions

It takes the combined efforts of many people to challenge gender stereotypes. Women and girls should be presented in a variety of sports roles, ranging from athletes to coaches and administrators, and the media, sports organizations, and individuals should all make a conscientious effort to destroy stereotypes and do so.

Offer Examples of Strong Women to Look Up to

It is imperative that the accomplishments of female athletes who serve as role models be brought to light and celebrated. Athletes, particularly female athletes, have the power to encourage others to participate in sports and to break down obstacles.

Encourage women to pursue careers in coaching and officiating

It is critical to inspire more women to work in sports at the administrative, coaching, and officiating levels of the industry. Women in positions of leadership within sports organizations contribute to the creation of more welcoming competition settings and offer prospective female athletes positive examples to aspire to.

Scholarships and grants should be made available

The availability of financial aid in the form of scholarships and grants for female athletes can assist lower the overall cost of participation. An effective way to encourage women and girls of all ages to participate in sports is to open up doors that lead to educational and athletic development opportunities.

Honor and recognize the accomplishments of women

It is imperative that the accomplishments of women and girls in the sporting world be recognized and celebrated. Others are inspired to participate when their accomplishments and efforts are brought to others' attention.

Participate Family Members

The encouragement of women and girls to take part in sporting activities is largely driven by the

actions of their families. It is important for parents, siblings, and other guardians to offer support, encouragement, and access to sporting activities for their children.

It's not only about the games when it comes to encouraging women and girls to get involved in athletics; it's also about developing individuals who are resilient, healthy, confident, and empowered, and who challenge gender stereotypes and advocate for gender equality. It demands a determined effort on the part of society as a whole, as well as sporting groups, educational institutions, families, and individuals. We can give women and girls the ability to reach their full potential on and off the field by removing the obstacles that have traditionally served to restrict their involvement in sports and by cultivating conditions that are welcoming to all members of the community. The positive effects of this empowerment extend far beyond the realm of athletics, making for a world that is more egalitarian and inclusive for everyone.

Chapter 8

The Role of Coaching and Training

Personal growth and success in multiple facets of life can be significantly aided by coaching and training in their respective spheres. Effective coaching and well-structured training programs can have a substantial influence on an individual's development, the learning of skills, and the accomplishment of their objectives, regardless of the context (e.g., sports, career, personal relationships, or any other field). In this extensive essay, we will investigate the complex role of coaching and training, diving into the significance of these activities as well as their methodologies, the benefits they provide, and the applications they find in a variety of fields.

1. **The Value of Having a Coach and Participating in Training**
   The Meaning of the Terms "Coaching" and "Training"
   Coaching and training are two distinct but closely linked practices that try to guide individuals to attain specific goals and enhance their skills and knowledge. The purpose of both coaching and training is to improve an individual's abilities and knowledge. While coaching frequently focuses on personal and professional growth, training typically places a greater emphasis on the acquisition of skills and the increase of one's knowledge. Both are necessary for one's own development and for achieving one's goals.

   Improvement of Oneself
   The capacity of coaching and training to motivate individuals toward self-improvement is one of the key justifications for its necessity. They assist people in determining their capabilities and limitations, in establishing objectives for themselves, and in formulating plans to overcome challenges and realize their full potential.

   Developing One's Capabilities
   To be successful in many other arenas, including athletics, business, and the arts, one needs to possess specialized abilities. Coaching and training programs that are effective give individuals with structured direction and practice to aid

in the process of acquiring and honing these abilities, which ultimately leads to improved performance and proficiency.

Accomplishment of Objectives

Coaching and training provide a structured framework that can be used for goal-setting and goal-accomplishment. The direction and accountability that are provided by coaches and trainers considerably boost the likelihood of success, regardless of whether the goals in question pertain to one's personal life, one's professional life, or one's athletic accomplishments.

Responsibility and Obtaining Feedback

Interaction with mentors, coaches, or trainers on a consistent basis is required for coaching and training. Individuals are held responsible for ensuring that they continue to make progress toward their goals and that they receive helpful feedback in order to effect any necessary modifications and improvements.

2. **The Practices Employed in Coaching and Instruction**

Personal Instruction One-on-One

In personalized one-on-one coaching, a coach works closely with an individual to give the latter with feedback and direction that is specific to their needs. This strategy is useful for resolving particular issues that may arise in one's work or personal life.

Coaching for Groups

Individuals who share objectives or struggles are encouraged to participate in a group setting for coaching. Participants are able to gain knowledge from one another, share their own experiences, and receive direction from a coach who moderates the group talks that take place.

Coaching Conducted Via the Internet

As a result of the proliferation of digital technology, more and more people are opting to receive coaching services online. The ability for clients and coaches to communicate online, whether through video conferences, emails, or messaging apps, broadens the pool of people who can benefit from coaching.

Various Seminars & Workshops

Training workshops and seminars give participants structured learning experiences, which can be used for the improvement of skills and the acquisition of new knowledge. They frequently include learning reinforcement activities such as lectures, interactive activities, and practical exercises.

Electronic Learning and Instructional Courses

E-learning platforms and online courses give users the ability to learn new skills and information at their own speed, making them more convenient than traditional classroom settings. Learners located all over the world benefit from these platforms' adaptability and accessibility.

Training through one's own efforts:

Apprenticeships are a time-honored method of instruction in many professions, including those in the trades and crafts. An apprentice is someone who works closely with an experienced mentor in order to obtain hands-on experience and learn specific skills.

Working Out and Practicing Your Skills

Training in sports and other physically demanding activities typically consists of a mix of different types of workouts, including drills and practice sessions, with the goal of improving overall performance and gaining greater control over skills.

3. **The Many Advantages That Come With Coaching and Training**

Enhanced Capability to Acquire Skills

Training programs offer a structured environment in which participants can acquire and develop a variety of abilities. Coaching and training can speed up the process of acquiring new skills, whether those skills are related to learning a musical instrument, enhancing communication in the office, or sharpening athletic ability.

Enhanced levels of both knowledge and expertise

Training is an essential factor in the development of one's knowledge and expertise. It provides people with the information and insight that they need to make educated decisions, find solutions to issues, and flourish in the profession that they have chosen for themselves.

Growth and Development on a Personal Level

Individuals are able to recognize their strengths and shortcomings, create personal objectives, and develop ways to overcome barriers with the assistance of a coach, which is one way that coaching encourages personal growth. It helps one become more self-aware as well as emotionally intelligent.

The importance of both Motivation and Accountability

The motivation and accountability that come from coaching and training come from the regular contacts that participants have with their mentors and trainers. Individuals are able to maintain their concentration and dedication to their objectives with the help of this support system.

Performance That Is Much Better

The majority of the time, coaching and training will result in an improvement in performance. In athletics, competitors try to reach their full potential in terms of performance, while in the business, employees strive to improve their level of productivity and efficiency.

Self-Respect and Confidence in Oneself

It is common for people's self-esteem and confidence to increase as they learn new abilities and expand their knowledge base. They will feel a sense of success and an increase in their self-confidence, both of which will benefit them in their personal and professional lives.

Clarity and the Establishment of Goals

Individuals can develop clarity about their goals and set goals that are more attainable with the assistance of coaching. Because of this procedure, students will maintain their concentration and motivation, and they will have a distinct plan for achieving their goals.

Improved Capacity for Making Decisions

Individuals are better equipped to make decisions that are in their best interests when they gain both their knowledge and their self-awareness. Training programs that provide an emphasis on critical thinking and problem-solving abilities help to improved decision-making.

Developing Leadership Skills

The development of leadership skills is significantly aided by coaching and various types of leadership training programs. They assist individuals in developing skills that are needed for leadership responsibilities, such as effective communication, decision-making, and conflict resolution, and they do so by providing opportunities for such development.

4. **Practical Applications of Mentoring and Instruction**

Aspects of Sport

Coaching is absolutely necessary in sports for the growth of athletes, the advancement of their skills, and their overall performance. The role of a coach is to provide advice and instruction to individual athletes as well as entire teams in all facets of a particular sport.

Commerce and managerial authority

The corporate sector makes extensive use of coaching as a means to encourage the development of leadership qualities, strengthen managerial abilities, and boost employee performance. Executives and managers frequently participate in leadership coaching in order to hone their leadership skills and become more effective leaders.

To educate

The field of education places a significant emphasis on coaching and mentoring. They assist students with developing effective study habits, overcoming obstacles in their academic work, and getting ready for tests. Academic coaching is a form of support that is offered to students who are working toward degrees in higher education.

Growth on a Personal Level

Life coaching is a common type of coaching that places an emphasis on the client's personal growth and the achievement of life goals. Coaches collaborate with their clients to strengthen connections, define and accomplish personal goals, and improve their clients' well-being in general.

Developing Your Profession

Individuals can benefit from making career selections, expanding their professional horizons, and advancing in their chosen professions with the assistance of a career coach. It provides direction on how to seek for jobs, how to prepare for interviews, and how to plan a career.

Conditioning and Well-Being

Personal trainers and health coaches offer advice to clients on how to improve their physical fitness, dietary habits, and general well-being. They assist clients in achieving their desired levels of fitness, losing weight, and living a healthy lifestyle overall.

The Creative Arts and Related Fields

In the creative areas, such as music, art, and literature, coaching and training are absolutely necessary. In order to hone their craft and improve their performance, musicians work with music teachers, artists seek out art teachers, and writers participate in writing workshops.

Relationships with other people

Relationship coaching is frequently sought out by couples who wish to enhance their communication and triumph over obstacles in their relationships. Coaches offer advice and direction to clients on how to develop strong, successful partnerships.

5. Obstacles and Things to Take Into Account

Credentials and Professional Accreditation

Due to the absence of regulated credentials and accreditation in the coaching and training sector, it is vital for customers and learners to conduct extensive research and select certified coaches and trainers.

Cost

The expense of coaching and training programs can be prohibitive, making participation in such endeavors difficult for persons who have restricted access to financial resources. One factor that needs to be taken into account in order to guarantee inclusion is the question of how much coaching and training cost.

Responsibility and a Focus on Quality

The quality and accountability of coaching and training programs are both need to be kept at a high standard. In order to assure the efficacy of this, continuous evaluation and feedback are required.

Variability at the Individual Level

Methods of coaching and training should be flexible enough to accommodate the unique requirements and educational preferences of each participant. It's important to tailor solutions to each individual's needs because what works for one person might not work for another.

Both coaching and training are extremely useful tools for fostering personal growth and achieving success in a variety of aspects of one's life. They provide systematic coaching, the acquisition of skills, enhancement of knowledge, and personal development opportunities. It is impossible to exaggerate the significance of coaching and training because they both offer a route to individual growth and the accomplishment of one's objectives.

It is essential to address the problems associated with qualifications, cost, responsibility, and individual variability as the industry of coaching and training continues to undergo significant change. Individuals will have the ability to attain their full potential and constructively contribute to society if we accomplish this because we will have ensured that coaching and training will continue to be available and effective. It doesn't matter if you're talking about athletics, business, education, or your own personal growth and development; the function of coaching and training is still essential to sculpting a better and more prosperous future.

8.1 The impact of professional coaching

The practice of professional coaching as a transforming force in personal and professional development, which assists individuals and organizations in reaching their full potential, has been increasingly popular in recent years. Professional coaching has been shown to be a key factor in successful outcomes across many different domains, including business, leadership, sports, and personal development. In this all-encompassing paper, we will look into the tremendous impact that professional coaching has, analyzing its significance, methodology, benefits, and applications across a wide range of industries.

1. Acquiring a Knowledge of Professional Coaching
   The Meaning of the Term "Professional Coaching"
   A certified coach works with an individual or team to improve performance, drive personal and professional growth, and accomplish particular goals in the context of professional coaching, which is a collaborative and goal-oriented approach. In order to assist their clients in realizing their full potential, coaches make use of a wide array of strategies, methodologies, and instruments.
   The Function of an Experienced and Qualified Coach
   A professional coach serves as a guide and a facilitator for their clients, assisting them in defining their objectives, recognizing potential roadblocks, formulating solutions, and overcoming obstacles. Clients are able to explore their potential and make progress toward their goals in an environment that is structured, supportive, and free from judgment thanks to the services provided by the coach.

2. The Effects of Working with a Professional Coach
   Growth on a Personal Level
   Personal development can be dramatically accelerated through the process of coaching. It assists people in developing a more in-depth awareness of themselves, their values, and the goals they aspire to achieve. As a direct consequence of this, clients frequently report greater levels of both self-awareness and self-confidence, as well as emotional intelligence.
   Developing Leadership Skills

The growth of leaders is greatly aided by the process of coaching. It helps leaders develop their interpersonal skills, as well as their communication, decision-making, and problem-solving abilities. Coaching helps leaders improve their effectiveness as well as their ability to inspire others and adapt to changing circumstances.

Performance That Is Much Better

The performance of athletes is considerably improved by professional coaching. Athletes, businessmen, artists, and others working in a variety of other industries have all experienced extraordinary growth in their talents, allowing them to achieve brilliance in their particular fields.

Accomplishment of Objectives

The process of defining and achieving goals is made easier by the structure provided by coaching. Clients collaborate with coaches to establish goals that are distinct and attainable, and coaches assist clients in maintaining accountability and remaining on track to achieve these objectives.

Communication that is Clear and Concise

The development of better communication skills is frequently a primary focus of coaching. Whether it be in personal relationships or at work, improved communication leads to improved collaboration, more effective resolution of conflicts, and more overall performance.

The Settlement of Conflicts

Professional coaches offer assistance to individuals and teams in the process of conflict resolution by enabling constructive communication, assisting parties in better understanding each other's points of view, and locating solutions that ultimately result in harmonious relationships.

Reduced levels of stress

Individuals receive the tools, tactics, and techniques necessary to control their stress, as well as coping mechanisms, through the process of coaching. This is especially helpful in high-pressure professional settings.

Progression in One's Profession

Individuals who are interested in advancing their careers may benefit from receiving coaching since it can offer them with the direction and strategy they need to navigate the professional environment, make well-informed career decisions, and accomplish their career goals.

Development of Businesses and Organizations

The expansion of businesses and organizations can also be influenced by professional coaching. It assists businesses in improving leadership, the dynamics of teams, and employee performance, which ultimately leads to an improvement in production and profitability.

The Process of Transforming and Changing

The process of coaching is beneficial to both individual and organizational growth. It gives people and organizations the capabilities they need to adjust to new circumstances, be open to new ideas, and flourish in contexts that are always shifting.

3. Strategies and Procedures Utilized in Professional Coaching

Coaching With a Focus on Goals

SMART objectives are goals that are specific, measurable, realistic, relevant, and time-bound. Goal-oriented coaching entails setting SMART goals. The coaching process involves the client and the coach working together to define specific goals and devise actionable tactics to achieve those goals.

Coaching With a Focus on Clients' Strengths

Coaching that is focused on an individual's skills and talents looks for those strengths and talents and tries to capitalize on them. When clients focus on what they excel at, coaches are able to assist them in realizing their full potential.

Coaching for Transformative Change

The realms of personal and professional development are both explored in transformational coaching. It challenges individuals to investigate their own values, beliefs, and behaviors, which ultimately results in substantial personal development and alteration.

Coaching using a Cognitive-Behavioral Approach

The focus of cognitive-behavioral coaching is on modifying both habitual patterns of thought and action. Together with their clients, coaches assist individuals recognize and reframe problematic thought patterns and behaviors, which ultimately results in positive change.

Coaching for Executives

The executives and managers of a company are the target audience for executive coaching. The development of leadership and management abilities, such as decision-making, communication, and team building, are the primary emphases of this program.

Coaching for a Lifetime

The process of life coaching takes a comprehensive approach and considers all aspects of an individual's life at the same time. It improves clients' overall well-being, helps them find balance in their personal and professional lives, and sets personal and professional goals.

Coaching for Teams and Groups

Working with a team or group to improve their performance in areas such as collaboration and

communication is what is meant by team and group coaching. The processes of group problem-solving and group dynamics can be facilitated by coaches.

Training for Emotional and Social Intelligence

Individuals can improve their emotional awareness, empathy, and social skills with the assistance of coaches who specialize in emotional intelligence. Clients are taught by coaches how to better comprehend and control the emotions that they experience.

4. The Numerous Advantages and Potential Fields of Application of Professional Coaching

Coaching for Leadership Positions and Executives

Leadership development and executive coaching equip executives with the skills necessary to make strategic decisions, to lead their teams successfully, and to cultivate a positive culture in the workplace. It improves their capacity to inspire and motivate teams, which in turn contributes to the success of the organization as a whole.

Career Counseling Services

Individuals can benefit from making informed career decisions, successfully navigating employment changes, and developing in their chosen profession with the assistance of career coaching. It offers advice on how to seek for a job, how to prepare for an interview, and how to plan a career.

Instruction in Athletics

The role of sports coaching in enhancing athletic performance cannot be overstated. Athletes collaborate with their coaches to hone their talents, define their performance objectives, and build mental toughness, all of which are necessary for achieving success in competitive sports.

Coaching for Individuals and Their Lives

Individuals are able to better create and achieve personal objectives, navigate life transitions, strengthen relationships, and improve their overall well-being with the assistance of personal and life coaching. It helps cultivate a sense of self-awareness, as well as confidence and fulfillment in one's life.

Coaching for Organizations and Individual Teams

Coaching at the organizational and team level covers issues relating to the dynamics of teams, leadership, and the performance of employees. It assists firms in improving their overall performance as well as productivity and innovation.

Instruction in the Subjects

The purpose of academic coaching is to provide students with assistance in the development of effective study skills, time management methods, and academic success tactics. It contributes to the improvement of learning and the accomplishment of educational objectives.

Coaching for Better Health and Wellness

The goal of health and wellness coaching is to assist individuals in making positive adjustments to their lifestyles, improving their ability to handle stress, and enhancing their overall health and well-being. Wellness coaches help their clients improve both their physical and mental health by working together.

5. Assessing the Results Obtained Through Professional Coaching

Evaluation by Oneself

Clients are able to conduct their own self-evaluations of their progress by contemplating their objectives, achievements, and potential for growth. They are able to monitor their own personal progress and advancement.

Feedback on a 360-Degree Scale

In the context of a business setting, receiving feedback from a client's superiors, peers, and subordinates is what is meant by "360-degree feedback." This feedback is then used to evaluate the client's performance and progress. The impact that coaching has had on a person's leadership abilities can be evaluated with the use of this feedback.

Assessments both before and after the event

Assessing a client's performance, knowledge, or abilities both before and after receiving coaching requires doing both pre and post assessments. These evaluations offer measurable evidence of the progress that has been made.

Indicators of Key Performance (also known as KPIs)

When it comes to business and organizational coaching, key performance indicators (KPIs) can be used to monitor changes in a variety of areas, including productivity, employee engagement, customer satisfaction, and financial performance.

Surveys of Customers' Levels of Satisfaction

Collecting feedback from customers in the form of customer satisfaction surveys allows for a more accurate assessment of the clients' overall experiences as well as the perceived influence of coaching on the clients' personal or professional growth.

6. Obstacles and Things to Take Into Account

Standards and Eligibility Requirements

Because there are no universally recognized credentials or accreditations in the coaching profession, it is vital for clients to do their own research and choose coaches who are competent and who abide by ethical norms.

Integrity of Behavior

The ethical conduct of a coach must be upheld at all times, and this includes maintaining client confidentiality, trust, and concern for their clients' well-being. It is essential for the coaching industry to ensure that ethical principles are followed.

Cost

Because of the potential high expense involved, people and organizations with limited financial means may find it difficult to obtain professional coaching. Taking steps to make things more affordable is a crucial step toward assuring inclusivity.

The Process of Coaching

The process of coaching is extremely individualized, and its effectiveness is contingent not only on the client's willingness to engage actively in the process but also on the compatibility of the coaching relationship. The strategy that coaches take must be modified to suit the requirements of each individual client.

A strong catalyst for personal and professional development, professional coaching is now helping individuals and companies attain their full potential and excel in their respective fields. It has a significant influence, having an effect on a variety of domains including athletics, personal development, professional advancement, and leadership.

It is vital to handle the problems connected to qualifications, ethical conduct, cost, and the individualized character of the coaching process. Professional coaching offers a great number of benefits; however, these challenges must first be addressed. We can ensure that professional coaching continues to be a transforming force for individuals and organizations that want to achieve new levels of achievement and personal fulfillment if we take these steps. As the coaching profession continues to develop, there is no end to the possibilities that it may bring about in terms of a better and more prosperous future.

8.2 Coaching techniques for physical and mental well-being

The quest of well-being must take into account both one's bodily and one's mental state because of the intricate connections that exist between the two. A holistic approach that takes into account both the body and the mind is required in order to realize the goals of attaining balance, contentment, and vitality. Techniques used in coaching that are aimed to improve a person's physical and mental well-being play an important part in directing people toward their ideal state of health and happiness. The purpose of this paper is to investigate coaching strategies that foster holistic well-being, with a particular emphasis on physical fitness, stress management, and mental toughness.

1. **Taking a Holistic Approach to One's Health and Wellness**

   The term "well-being" refers to a state of overall happiness and contentment with one's life, as well as one's bodily and mental health, emotional stability, and balance, and overall life satisfaction. The interconnectedness of both components is acknowledged by a holistic approach, which then works to develop both of them at the same time.

   Wellness in terms of one's body

   Maintaining a healthy body can be accomplished by consuming nutritious foods, engaging in regular physical activity, getting sufficient sleep, and receiving necessary medical attention. It is the basis upon which a person's mental and emotional well-being can develop and grow.

   The state of one's mind

   Emotional stability, cognitive performance, and psychological fortitude are the three aspects of mental health that make up well-being. Stress management, the cultivation of positive thought patterns, and the development of emotional intelligence are all included in this process.

Harmony of the Feelings

Emotional balance refers to an individual's capacity to comprehend, acknowledge, and skillfully control their feelings. Developing one's emotional intelligence is necessary for fostering healthy relationships and successfully navigating the obstacles that life throws to us, and this aspect of oneself must be cultivated.

Contentment with One's Life

The underlying feeling of pleasure and fulfillment that people experience in their lives is referred to as life satisfaction. It is impacted by the equilibrium and concordance that exists between a person's physical, mental, and emotional well-being.

2. **Techniques of Coaching for Physical Health and Wellness**

Techniques used in coaching that focus on the physical well-being of athletes include the promotion of a healthy lifestyle that includes appropriate nutrition, adequate rest, and adequate physical activity. People who are interested in improving their physical health might receive assistance and support by utilizing these strategies.

Setting Objectives

The establishment of goals is an essential part of the coaching process. The term "specific," "measurable," "attainable," "relevant," and "time-bound" (SMART) refers to goals that are set by individuals with the assistance of coaches. These goals relate to the individual's physical well-being and may include things like weight loss, muscle gain, or improved cardiovascular health.

Instruction in Nutritional Matters

Nutritional coaching is provided by coaches, assisting customers in making well-informed decisions on their dietary habits. This may involve coming up with meal planning, learning how to read nutrition labels, and gaining an awareness of how much food to consume.

The Planning of Physical Activity

Creating an organized fitness program that is in line with the client's goals and preferences is an important part of the planning process for physical exercise. The development of workout regimens, the monitoring of progress, and the provision of inspiration are all tasks that are assisted by coaches.

Taking responsibility

Clients are held accountable by coaches for achieving the goals they set for their physical well-being. The customers benefit from having regular check-ins and progress assessments performed, as this helps them stay on track with their health and fitness routines and maintains their level of dedication.

The Management of Stress

Techniques for managing stress are essential to maintaining one's physical health. Clients are guided by coaches through the process of stress management using techniques such as mindfulness, deep breathing, and progressive muscle relaxation.

3. **Techniques for Coaching that Promote Mental Health and Well-Being**

   Enhancing cognitive performance, emotional control, and psychological resilience are the primary focuses of coaching methods for mental well-being. Individuals can improve their mental fortitude and emotional equilibrium with the help of these approaches.

   Reorganization of Thought Processes

   The process of identifying and addressing unhelpful thought patterns and beliefs that have a role in mental health conditions such as stress, anxiety, and depression is known as cognitive restructuring. Clients often benefit from having their thinking reframed by coaches into patterns that are more positive and helpful.

   Meditation and a focus on the present moment

   Meditation and mindfulness activities help people become more self-aware and better able to control their emotions. Mindfulness training helps individuals acquire the ability to be present in the moment and take control of their feelings with the guidance of a coach.

   Psychology of the Positive

   Techniques from the field of positive psychology are centered on the cultivation of positive emotions and strengths. Coaches assist their clients in recognizing and capitalizing on their individual qualities, which in turn cultivates resiliency, optimism, and a sense of life satisfaction.

   Intelligence pertaining to the emotions

   The goal of emotional intelligence coaching is to help clients have a better awareness of and control over their feelings and behaviors. The goal of coaching is to help clients become more self-aware, empathic, and effective in their interactions with others.

   Techniques for Alleviating the Effects of Stress

   Stress reduction approaches, such as time management, relaxation methods, and assertiveness training are some of the topics that coaches cover with their clients. Individuals are better able to cope with the pressures of day-to-day living and experience less stress as a result of using these tactics.

4. **Methods of Coaching for Maintaining Emotional Balance**

   Individuals are better able to comprehend, accept, and effectively control their emotions with the support of coaching strategies for emotional balance. These methods help people develop their emotional intelligence and strengthen their relationships with others.

   Exercises in Personal Introspection

   Individuals can obtain insight into their emotional responses and triggers as well as their emotional experiences by engaging in self-reflective exercises, which allow individuals to investigate their emotional experiences, recognize patterns, and identify patterns.

Keeping a journal

Writing in a journal is an effective method for processing one's feelings and for introspection. Journals provide patients with an outlet to process their feelings, keep a gratitude log, and monitor their own personal improvement.

Competences in the Resolution of Conflict

Skills for resolving conflicts, such as effective communication, active listening, and negotiating strategies, are among the topics that coaches teach their students. These abilities contribute to the development of stronger connections with others.

Emotional Control or Management

Individuals can better regulate intense emotions and avoid becoming emotionally overwhelmed by employing approaches for emotional regulation. Techniques such as taking slow, deep breaths, performing grounding exercises, and other forms of self-soothing activities are taught by coaches.

5. **Methods of Coaching to Achieve Greater Life Satisfaction**

The strategies of life satisfaction coaching are geared toward assisting individuals in achieving a state of contentment and fulfillment in their lives. These practices encourage an optimistic view, an attitude of appreciation, and a sense of purpose in one's life.

Clarification of Core Values

Clarification of values helps individuals understand their essential values, which serve as a compass for making decisions about one's life and developing meaningful goals that match with one's values. Values can also be defined as a person's "guiding principles."

The Training of Gratitude

Recognizing and appreciating the positive parts of one's life on a regular basis is an essential component of the gratitude practice. The practice of expressing thankfulness regularly has shown to be associated with a more optimistic frame of mind.

Meaning and Direction in One's Life

Clients are guided by coaches through the process of developing a life vision and mission statement, which helps clients gain clarity regarding their life objectives, aspirations, and the legacy they hope to leave behind.

Compassion for Oneself

Individuals can learn to treat themselves with kindness through the use of strategies known as self-compassion, which are particularly helpful during difficult circumstances. It assists people in overcoming their own self-criticism and in developing their sense of self-worth.

6. **The Influence That Coaching Methods Have On A Holistic Level**

Improved Overall Quality of Life

The use of coaching strategies can lead to an improvement in one's quality of life. People report feeling happier and more satisfied with their lives overall. They also report having more vigor.

Enhancement of One's Physical Condition

The application of coaching strategies for physical well-being leads to improvements in one's physical health, such as better control of one's weight, enhanced cardiovascular health, and enhanced overall fitness.

Reduced Levels of Anxiety and Stress

The levels of stress and anxiety can be lowered by the use of coaching approaches for mental well-being and stress management. Clients learn to be resilient and build coping techniques to help them deal with the difficulties of life.

Enhanced Capacity to Regulate Emotions

The development of healthier emotional reactions and interpersonal interactions can be fostered through the application of techniques that promote emotional balance and awareness of one's own emotions.

Optimistic view on things

The strategies of life satisfaction coaching help clients cultivate a more optimistic attitude on life, which in turn contributes to their overall sense of well-being and fulfillment.

7. **Difficulties and Things to Think About**

Although there are many advantages to be gained from using coaching methods for one's wellbeing, there are also many problems and factors to take into mind.

Variation at the Individual Level

The methods of coaching must be modified to accommodate the specific requirements, preferences, and openness to change of each client. What is successful for one individual might not be so successful for another.

Considerations of an Ethical Nature

The coach has a responsibility to respect ethical norms in order to ensure that the client-coach relationship is founded on trust, confidentiality, and the client's overall well-being.

Harmony with One's Own Personal Values

It is important for coaching methods to be congruent with an individual's fundamental ideas and values in order to guarantee that the tactics are personally relevant and inspiring.

A Dedication to Making Changes

The client must be willing to actively participate in the coaching process and be committed to achieving the goals they have set for their own well-being. For there to be any real change, work and dedication are required.

A holistic approach to personal development and living a life that is fulfilling can be represented by the coaching strategies that promote physical and mental health. These strategies target the interrelated dimensions of well-being, such as one's physical health, emotional equilibrium, cognitive performance, and overall level of life satisfaction. Coaching helps individuals pursue well-being and realize their entire mental and physical potential by supplying them with direction, support, and a methodical approach. This encourages individuals to realize their full potential in both areas.

It is becoming increasingly clear that the coaching profession has the ability to help individuals design a future that is both brighter and healthier as it continues to develop.

Those who adopt coaching strategies aimed to promote their physical and mental well-being, fostering happiness, vitality, and enduring contentment, have a better chance of living a life that is well-balanced and full to the extent that it is within their reach.

8.3 The ethics of coaching and mentoring

Coaching and mentoring are practices that have their origins deeply ingrained in the guiding, supporting, and growing of others ideals. As a result of this, upholding ethical norms is essential to developing a trustworthy and productive relationship for the purposes of mentoring or coaching. By upholding ethical principles, coaches and mentors guarantee that they will put the health and development of their clients or mentees first, which in turn helps to create an atmosphere that is both helpful and professional. We will examine the major ethical concepts that underlie coaching and mentoring in this essay, with a particular emphasis on the necessity of trust, integrity, and professionalism in these partnerships.

1. **Integrity and Private Conversations**

   Developing a trustworthy relationship is essential to the success of any mentoring or coaching endeavor. In order for clients or mentees to feel at ease discussing their thoughts, concerns, and goals without the worry of being judged or having their anonymity compromised, coaches and mentors are tasked with the responsibility of establishing a secure and discrete environment. It is essential to show customers or mentees that you respect their right to privacy in order to establish trust and keep up a supportive environment that encourages open communication and personal development.

2. **Respect for One's Own Independence and Boundaries**

   It is crucial to both coaching and mentoring to respect the autonomy of the people being coached or mentored. The individual's right to make their own decisions and choices should be respected by coaches and mentors, and individuals should be guided without having their own views or values imposed on them. It is absolutely necessary, in order to maintain a professional and ethical mentoring or coaching relationship, to respect the personal limits of the person being coached or mentored and to avoid any type of manipulation or coercion.

3. **Honesty and Dedication to the Profession**

   When it comes to mentoring and coaching, two of the most important ethical standards are integrity and professionalism. It is required of coaches and mentors to behave in an honest, transparent, and accountable manner. They should also make sure that their activities are aligned with what is in the best interests of their customers or mentees. The maintenance of high ethical standards helps to cultivate an environment that is professional and trustworthy, which contributes to the overall success and efficiency of the mentoring or coaching relationship.

4. **Approach that is Both Non-Judgmental and Non-Discriminationary**

   In the fields of coaching and mentoring, it is essential to take an approach that is nondiscriminatory and free of judgment. Respect for diversity, cultural variations, and unique perspectives should be exhibited by coaches and mentors in order to foster an environment that is welcoming and encouraging to clients or mentees who come from a variety of backgrounds. It is vital to adopt a position that is neither judgmental nor discriminatory in order to facilitate the development of rapport, as well as a sense of acceptance and comprehension, within the context of the mentoring or coaching relationship.

5. **Competence, as well as ongoing Development**

   It is a vital ethical responsibility for coaches and mentors to continue their professional education and education in general in order to maintain their level of competence. It is essential for coaches and mentors to remain current with the most recent practices, theories, and approaches in the field of mentoring and coaching in order to provide their customers or mentees with accurate and pertinent guidance. The demonstration of a passion to providing high-quality coaching and mentoring services while keeping to ethical standards is demonstrated by making a commitment to continual learning and development.

6. **Consent Given After Understanding Risks and Communicating Clearly**

   The ethical requirements of coaching and mentoring include obtaining informed permission and ensuring clear communication at all times. It is the responsibility of coaches and mentors to ensure that the people they are working with have a comprehensive understanding of the coaching or mentoring process, including its goals, techniques, and potential results. Communication that is both open and transparent helps to encourage mutual understanding and collaboration, which in turn enables clients or mentees to take an active role in the development of their own personal and professional lives.

7. **Making Ethical Decisions and Resolving Conflicts with Others**

The ability to make decisions in an ethical manner and effectively resolve conflicts is an essential talent for coaches and mentors. When confronted with difficult circumstances or ethical conundrums, coaches and mentors should put the health and happiness of their charges and the achievement of their goals ahead of their own concerns. The demonstration of a commitment to respecting professional standards and encouraging positive results in the coaching or mentoring relationship is demonstrated by the application of ethical principles to the resolution of conflicts and the making of informed judgments.

Chapter 9

Balancing Cricket with Other Aspects of Life

Players in the sport of cricket, which is both physically demanding and time-consuming, are frequently need to establish a fine balance between their athletic aspirations and other important elements of their lives. It doesn't matter if it's your schooling, your work, your family, or your personal interests; striking a balance that's both harmonious and balanced is essential to your general well-being and continued success. This essay examines the complex nature of juggling cricket with other elements of life, focusing on the significance of effective time management, holistic growth, and the creation of supporting environments.

1. **Being Aware of the Demands That Cricket Places On You**
   The Commitment of Time, as well as Training
   The sport of cricket requires a large time commitment due to the strenuous training sessions, practice matches, and competitions that are required. Players frequently devote a significant amount of time to developing their gaming abilities, physical fitness, and game techniques, which can limit their capacity to participate in additional activities.
   Both mental and physical fortitude are required.
   Cricket is a sport that requires players to have a high level of stamina, endurance, and focus at all times due to the mental and physical demands of the game. Keeping up with the mental pressure of competition while also keeping up with the physical demands of the game may be a difficult and stressful task.
   The World of Travel and Business
   As a result of the substantial travel required for matches, tournaments, and training camps, cricket players frequently spend extended amounts of time away from their homes and families. It can be difficult and emotionally stressful to maintain a healthy work-life balance while also meeting the demands of a competitive cricket career and other personal obligations.

2. **The Importance of Finding a Healthy Balance Between Cricket and Other Aspects of Your Life**

Growth on a Holistic Level

In order to develop on a holistic level, it is necessary to strike a balance between cricket and other elements of life. Outside of the realm of cricket, fostering well-rounded growth and a sense of contentment can be accomplished by participation in a variety of activities, such as education, career aspirations, and personal interests.

Planning Your Profession Over the Long Term

The ability to prepare for a long-term career beyond the active playing years of cricket requires players to strike a balance between cricket and other parts of life. Players can better prepare themselves for life after cricket by devoting time and energy to educational pursuits, the development of relevant skills, and the investigation of potential post-playing careers.

To be in good mental and emotional health

Maintaining a healthy mental and emotional state requires striking a balance between cricket and other aspects of life. Keeping a healthy work-life balance helps minimize stress, boosts general mood, and cultivates feelings of contentment and fulfillment.

Developing Solid Relationships as a Priority

Players who are able to strike a healthy balance between their personal lives and their cricket careers are better able to cultivate and sustain healthy connections with their families, friends, and peers. Outside of the confines of cricket, maintaining these connections provides essential emotional support and a sense of belonging to those involved.

3. **Methods for Maintaining a Healthy Balance Between Cricket and Other Aspects of Your Life**

Effective Management of One's Time

In order to maintain a healthy balance between cricket and other elements of life, it is essential to implement tactics for successful time management. Players are better able to balance their commitments to cricket, their education, their careers, and their personal lives when they use disciplined timetables, prioritize their activities, and set goals that are within their reach.

Defining Each Aspect's Role Precisely

It is absolutely necessary to establish distinct priorities in order to keep a healthy balance between cricket and other elements of one's life. Players are required to determine what aspects of their lives they value the most, whether it be academic success, professional promotion, or personal growth, and then direct their efforts appropriately.

Support and Open Lines of Communication

It is absolutely necessary to keep an open line of communication with one's coaches, teammates, and family members in order to successfully cultivate a supportive environment that makes room for both cricket and personal obligations. Players are more likely to pursue a balanced lifestyle if they have established a solid support structure for themselves.

Pursuing Educational Opportunities and Developing One's Skills

It is possible for players to better prepare themselves for post-cricket job options by placing a

greater emphasis on the value of education and skill development alongside sport. Players have a variety of alternatives available to them for their future pursuits if they choose to pursue further education, vocational training, or skill enhancement programs.

Acceptance of Sleep and Recuperation

It is essential to make recuperation and relaxation a top priority in order to preserve both one's physical and mental health. In order for players to recover from the mental and physical demands of cricket, adequate rest intervals, relaxation techniques, and stress-reduction measures are all beneficial. These help players maintain their overall health and vigor.

4. **Striking a Balance Between Education and a Career While Playing Cricket**

Education as a Crucial Building Block

Cricket players are given a solid academic foundation that bolsters their personal and professional development when there is an emphasis placed on the relevance of education alongside the sport of cricket. Education fosters analytical thinking, skills for problem solving, and intellectual development, all of which contribute to an overall improvement in a player's cognitive abilities.

Academic Activities That Allow for Flexibility

Players are able to better match their cricket responsibilities with their scholastic aspirations when their academic endeavors are allowed more leeway for flexibility. Players are able to manage their cricket careers while continuing their education thanks to flexible learning programs, distance education, and online courses.

Exploration of Professions and Continuing Education

Players will be better able to discover their interests, abilities, and potential future career routes if they are encouraged to explore and build their careers alongside their cricket play. Players are given the opportunity to gain useful insights and experiences outside of the sport of cricket through career advice, mentorship programs, and internships.

Preparing for Life After Cricket: Transition Planning

Players are more equipped for a successful and satisfying post-playing career if they are provided with assistance in transition planning for life beyond cricket. Participants can make a smooth transition into new professional jobs or entrepreneurial endeavors with the assistance of career workshops, skill development programs, and networking events.

5. **Cultivating Healthy Personal Relationships and a Positive State of Being**
The support of one's family and community
It is essential for one's mental health and sense of belonging to spend time cultivating personal relationships with members of one's family and circle of friends. Strong familial ties and meaningful social relationships can be fostered through consistent conversation and interaction, quality time spent together, and the exchange of experiences.

Care for Oneself and One's Mental Health
Putting one's mental health and self-care first is an effective way to foster emotional fortitude and psychological well-being. Outside of the game of cricket, players who want to properly manage their stress, anxiety, and emotional issues should participate in activities such as meditation, mindfulness techniques, and hobbies.

Integration of Work and Life
Players are able to balance their commitments to cricket with their personal interests and duties when there is a focus on integrating work and life. The cultivation of a balanced lifestyle that promotes general happiness and contentment can be facilitated by developing a synergistic relationship between cricket and one's personal life.

Participation in Community Activities and Volunteer Work
Players are able to contribute to society and have a beneficial impact beyond the boundaries of the cricket pitch if they are encouraged to get involved in their communities and volunteer their time. The cultivation of a sense of purpose and fulfillment can be accomplished by involvement in social causes, charitable activities, and community service initiatives.

6. **The Effects of Striking a Healthy Balance Between Cricket and Other Aspects of Life**
Improved Capability in All Aspects of Development
Developing a well-rounded personality requires a healthy mix of activities, and one of those activities should be cricket. Players who participate in a variety of activities display a stronger capacity for adaptability and resilience, as well as a more well-rounded outlook on life.

Career Achievement Over the Long Term
Creating a successful foundation for a long-term career in cricket requires striking a balance between sport and other elements of one's life. Players that place a high priority on education, the development of their skills, and the cultivation of personal relationships grow a robust support system and a diverse skill set that can propel them to success beyond the scope of their cricket careers.

Strength of Character and Emotional and Mental Health
Maintaining a healthy emotional and mental state requires striking a balance between one's professional and personal lives. Players who make taking care of

their mental health a priority and who cultivate and sustain healthy personal connections have a better degree of emotional intelligence, which has a beneficial effect on their overall performance and well-being.

Influence favorably exerted on the local community

Players who successfully juggle cricket with other activities, such as community service and support for social causes, contribute to the overall improvement of society. Their participation in community projects and volunteers is evidence of their dedication to social responsibility and inspires positive change within their own areas.

7. **Difficulties and Things to Think About**

In spite of the fact that juggling cricket with other elements of life can result in a number of positive outcomes, doing so is not without its share of difficulties and concerns.

Time Restriction Requirements and Obligations

The limitations on one's time and the requirements of playing cricket might make it difficult to balance other priorities, such as one's schooling, work, or personal interests. The players are required to strike a healthy work-life balance so that they can flourish in their cricketing careers as well as in other aspects of their lives.

Psychological and Emotional Exhaustion

The mental and emotional exhaustion that comes with trying to juggle cricket with other aspects of life can have a negative impact on a player's general well-being and performance. In order to keep a healthy equilibrium, it is vital to find effective ways to manage stress, anxiety, and mental tiredness.

Planning for the Transition

In order to successfully plan for life after cricket, much consideration and planning are required. To ensure a smooth transition into employment outside of playing, players need to put time and effort into improving their skills, furthering their education, and researching potential jobs.

Dealing with Accidents and Other Obstacles

sport players are susceptible to injuries and setbacks, which can throw off their equilibrium between sport and other elements of their lives. Players are required to cultivate mental and emotional coping techniques in order to successfully traverse hard situations and regain their equilibrium.

Finding a happy medium between playing cricket and committing time to other elements of your life is a difficult and multi-layered endeavor that calls for thoughtful deliberation, meticulous preparation, and unwavering dedication. Obtaining this equilibrium is necessary for one's own development, as well as for the duration of one's job and overall well-being. Players can achieve a state of harmonious equilibrium that enables them to excel both on and off the cricket field by practicing good time management, taking a holistic approach to their growth, and cultivating circumstances that are supportive of their efforts. Players have the opportunity to lead fulfilling lives that are well-rounded and contribute positively to their own growth as well as to the communities in which they live if they can successfully juggle cricket with other parts of life. This is not just a task; it's an opportunity.

9.1 Time management and prioritizing responsibilities

Time management and the ability to prioritize duties are two of the most important skills to have in order to be successful in both your personal and professional life. In today's fast-paced world, when the demands placed on our time appear to be unlimited, the ability to prioritize activities and responsibilities as well as good time management are absolutely necessary. In this paper, we will investigate the theories and methods of time management, investigate the process of prioritization, and talk about the influence that these abilities have on our lives and the things we want to do.

1. **Having a Good Handle on Your Time Management**
   The Meaning of the Term "Time Management"
   The process of planning and organizing how you will devote different portions of your time to different jobs and pursuits is referred to as time management. It include establishing goals, developing timetables, and employing a variety of tactics to achieve the highest possible levels of productivity and efficiency.
   How Valuable Your Time Is
   Time is a resource that has a limited supply and cannot be replenished. The ways in which we allot and manage our time have a significant impact on our capacity to achieve objectives, seek opportunities for personal growth, and lead lives that are both balanced and satisfying.
   The Catch-22 of Effective Time Management
   Even though many of us have the intention of improving our time management skills, doing so is not always easy to do. The paradox of time management is that the more we try to control and manage time, the more it can sometimes feel as if time is dominating us. This is especially true when we prioritize tasks that need a lot of attention to detail.

2. **The Core Concepts Behind Efficient Time Management**
   Setting Objectives
   The most important step in efficient time management is goal-setting that is both explicit and specific. Goals provide us a sense of direction, purpose, and drive, and they guide the allocation of our time to activities that are in line with our goals.
   Establishing Priorities
   The process of prioritization entails selecting the activities that are both the most important and the most urgent to work on first. It makes certain that your time is spent on activities that will have the most significant bearing on achieving your objectives.

The Processes of Planning and Scheduling

When you plan and schedule, you are essentially drawing up a road map for the day, the week, or even the year. It enables you to allot time to particular activities, preventing you from overlooking any essential responsibilities in the process.

Transfer of authority

The process of entrusting another person with a responsibility when you are confident in their ability to carry it out is known as delegation. Your time might be freed up for more important responsibilities when you delegate effectively.

Keeping Tabs on Time

The process of managing your time effectively requires that you keep track of how you spend your time. It assists you in identifying inefficiencies and places in which you could more effectively devote your time.

Attempts Made to Reduce Distractions

In this day and age, eliminating as many distractions as possible is really essential. Your productivity may suffer if you are not able to efficiently manage the steady stream of notifications, emails, and social media posts that come your way.

3. **Techniques for Efficient Time Management is the Third Section.**

The Eisenhower Reconstruction Matrix

The Eisenhower Matrix is a prioritization tool that divides activities into four quadrants based on their level of importance and urgency: important but not urgent, important but not urgent, neither urgent nor important, and neither urgent nor important. This enables you to concentrate on the things that are actually important.

The Technique of the Pomodoro

The Pomodoro Technique is a way for managing your time that involves segmenting your work into intervals of typically 25 minutes in duration, which are then followed by brief pauses in between each interval. It is possible for it to aid boost focus as well as productivity.

Blocking Out Time

The technique of allocating certain chunks of time on a schedule to carry out certain responsibilities or activities is referred to as "time blocking." It ensures that you give significant amounts of time to the responsibilities that are most essential to you.

Lists of Duties

The ability to organize and prioritize your activities on a daily or weekly basis is made possible when you create task lists or to-do lists. The satisfaction of crossing off finished chores on a list is a powerful motivator.

Applications and tools for time management

The process of time management can be made more efficient with the help of a variety of apps and tools for managing time, such as calendars, task organizers, and apps for creating goals.

4. **The Skill of Putting Things in Order of Importance**

Contrast "Importance" and "Urgency"

Not all responsibilities are equally pressing or crucial. It is essential to be able to differentiate between what should be given priority and what may be put off until later. Your immediate focus is required for jobs that are urgent, but the work you do that is vital makes a major contribution to the achievement of your long-term goals and your general well-being.

The Principle of 80/20

According to the Pareto Principle, sometimes known as the 80/20 rule, approximately 80% of your results come from only 20% of your efforts. But what does that mean? Putting a higher priority on the activities that make up this 20% of the total workload can lead to more substantial results.

The Affects and the Repercussions

Take into consideration the results and effects of each activity. While certain responsibilities may have far-reaching impacts, others may not be as important. Give the highest priority to the tasks that will either help you achieve your overall goals or will have severe repercussions if they are ignored.

Personal Values and Aims and Objectives

When you're trying to decide what to prioritize, it's important to take into account both your personal values and your long-term ambitions. It is important to give priority to the activities that are in line with your beliefs and help you work toward your goals.

Distribution of Resources

When prioritizing projects, make sure to take into account the resources you have available to you, such as time, energy, and talents. Make sure that you give priority to the responsibilities that will have the greatest impact on the organization.

5. **The Influence of Managing One's Time and Setting Priorities**

The ability to prioritize tasks and manage one's time efficiently can have a profound impact on one's personal and professional life.

Increased Effort and Output

Productivity can be considerably increased by assigning appropriate priorities to jobs and practicing good time management. You are able to get more done in the same amount of time, freeing up more time for other necessary responsibilities or enjoyable pursuits.

Reduced Levels of Stress

Managing one's time more effectively results in lower levels of stress and anxiety. The stress that results from putting things off till the last minute or rushing through them can be reduced if you plan ahead, divide up your work, and stick to your timetable.

A better balance between work and life

Through efficient time management and setting priorities, it is possible to strike a healthy balance between one's personal and professional lives. You have the ability to devote enough time to your loved ones, your hobbies, and yourself, which will result in a life that is more well-rounded and satisfying.

Achieving one's objectives

The successful accomplishment of your objectives is highly dependent on your ability to prioritize and efficiently manage your time. You have the ability to focus your time and energy on activities that make a direct contribution to achieving your goals, whether those goals are professional or personal in nature.

Enhanced Capability in Making Decisions

The process of prioritization helps you become better at making decisions. It assists you in evaluating tasks, deciding between options, and properly allocating resources, which ultimately leads to better decisions in both your personal and professional life.

6. **Obstacles and Things to Take Into Account**

Overcommitting oneself

When you take on too many projects and duties, it can be difficult to effectively manage your time. The ability to maintain a healthy work-life balance requires developing the skill of learning when and how to say "no."

Capacity for Change

It is essential to have the capacity to readjust one's priorities and adaptation strategies in response to unforeseen occurrences or crises. Having a strategy to managing your time and setting priorities that is both flexible and adaptable enables you to respond successfully to changing situations.

Care for Oneself

When trying to manage one's time more efficiently, it might be counterproductive to ignore one's own needs for self-care. It is essential to schedule time in one's schedule for relaxation, rest, and leisure activities in order to keep one's general health in good standing.

A Strive for Perfection

The pursuit of perfection can be detrimental to efficient time management. Over-committing oneself and experiencing stress that is not necessary might result when one strives for perfection in every endeavor. It is crucial to be able to recognize when "good enough" is sufficient.

The ability to prioritize one's tasks and manage one's time is a priceless asset that enables individuals to seize control of their life, realize their ambitions, and foster a feeling of well-being in themselves. You may increase your productivity, lower your stress levels, and keep a good work-life balance if you master the art of prioritization and adhere to the principles of successful time management. These competencies are not only useful in professional settings, but they also have a significant impact on your personal life and make it possible for you to live a life that is more satisfying and guided by a sense of purpose. To be successful in both one's personal and professional life in our fast-paced world, efficient time management and the ability to prioritize one's obligations are crucial tools.

9.2 Balancing cricket with work and education

In order to pursue a career in cricket, one must frequently juggle the demands of the sport with those of other commitments, such as employment and school. Cricket is a hobby for a lot of people, but it's not necessarily the only method to make money or the main thing people focus on in their lives. Individuals need to be able to successfully negotiate the complex juggling act that is cricket, work, and school in order to achieve overall success. In the following paragraphs, we will investigate the difficulties, possible solutions, and the relevance of achieving a healthy equilibrium between these three aspects of one's life.

1. **The Struggles Inherent in Juggling Cricket With Other Commitments Like Work And School**

   The Requirements of Time in Cricket

   A large time commitment is required to play cricket. A significant portion of an athlete's schedule may be taken up by practices, competitions, and other obligations related to their sport. It can be difficult to find a balance between all of these commitments, including employment and school.

   Uncertain Timing of Events

   The scheduling for cricket might be difficult to predict. It is difficult to organize employment or academic responsibilities with assurance when fixtures and competitions can be rescheduled or stretched out over a longer period of time.

   Stability in the Financial Sector

   Many cricket players, particularly those who are just starting out in their careers, may find that the sport does not provide a reliable or major source of revenue. For the sake of one's financial security, maintaining a healthy work-school balance is of paramount importance.

   Keeping Up with the Performance Levels

   Maintaining one's physical and mental health while playing cricket in addition to other obligations, such as work and school, can be challenging. Managing your time effectively is essential if you want to play at a high level in cricket while also fulfilling your other obligations.

2. **Methods for Maintaining a Healthy Balance Between Cricket, Work, and Education**

   Effective Management of One's Time

   To successfully juggle cricket, work, and schooling, efficient time management is absolutely necessary. Individuals are able to increase their productivity and lower their stress levels when they create timetables, establish priorities, and allot time to their many commitments.

Mobility and adaptability

To successfully navigate the unpredictability of cricket scheduling, flexibility is essential. Employers and educational institutions that are willing to be adaptable and accommodating can make a major difference in the difficulty of juggling several commitments.

Remote Work and Education Conducted Online

Those interested in pursuing careers in cricket now have access to valuable choices, including online schooling and remote work. Because of these arrangements, folks are able to work or study from any location, which makes it much simpler for them to organize their cricket schedules.

Look for Employers and Organizations That Will Support You.

Finding jobs and educational institutions that recognize the demands of a career in cricket and are willing to accept flexible scheduling is one way to significantly ease the balancing act.

Pursue Occupations That Are Of Use.

It may be useful to choose a job path that fits in well alongside a cricket career. Some people choose careers in the sports industry, like as coaching, sports management, or sports journalism, which enables them to maintain a close connection to the sport of cricket.

3. **The Importance of Striking a Balance Between Cricket, Your Other Activities, and Your Education**

Stability in the Financial Sector

Maintaining a stable financial situation requires striking a balance between playing cricket, working, and going to school. The financial unpredictability that is commonly associated with a career in cricket can be mitigated by having a reliable income from work or receiving financial support from education.

Planning for the Long Term

Individuals are better equipped to prepare for their lives after their cricket careers if they maintain a healthy work-school balance. It offers both a safety net and a basis for activities that can be pursued after retirement.

Growth on a Holistic Level

Maintaining a broad perspective while juggling various obligations is essential to growth. In addition to furthering their cricket careers, it affords athletes the opportunity to advance themselves in a variety of other spheres of life, such as their academic pursuits and personal growth.

To be in good mental and emotional health

Maintaining a healthy mental and emotional state requires striking a balance between one's various obligations. The tension and anxiety that are frequently experienced in cricket can be mitigated to some degree by diversifying one's concentration and hobbies, which eventually contributes to general pleasure.

Ability to be Flexible and Adaptable

The ability to be flexible and adaptable can be honed by playing cricket in addition to other commitments, such as job and school. These are transferable abilities that will serve you well not only in sports but in other facets of your life.

4. Obstacles and Things to Take Into Account

Administration of Time

It is essential to manage one's time well. To successfully manage a number of responsibilities, meticulous planning and scheduling are required to guarantee that each facet of one's life receives the appropriate amount of attention.

Tiredness, both mentally and physically

Trying to play cricket while also juggling job and school can be taxing on both your body and your mind. People need to take precautions to protect themselves against weariness and burnout.

Stability in the Financial Sector

Cricket may not always give a regular income, and it can be difficult to balance employment and school while still meeting financial obligations. It is critical to look for scholarship options as well as employers who will help you.

Mobility and adaptability

The ability to play cricket while juggling other commitments, such as job and school, requires employers and educational institutions to be flexible and tolerant. It might be a considerable issue to locate colleges or jobs that are willing to accommodate cricket players' schedules.

Maintaining a healthy work-life and school-life balance while playing cricket is a difficult challenge that calls for meticulous planning, unwavering commitment, and adaptability.

Despite the fact that a career in cricket can have demanding requirements, those who are able to effectively balance cricket, employment, and education frequently find that they are well-prepared for a life that is both enjoyable on and off the field of play. Individuals may traverse this precarious balancing act and prosper in their cricket careers while simultaneously safeguarding their futures outside of the sport if they seek out surroundings that are encouraging, become adept at managing their time, and embrace flexibility.

9.3 Maintaining relationships and social life

Maintaining healthy personal relationships while also having an active social life can be difficult in the fast-paced, hectic environment of modern living. It is easy for individuals to allow the links of friendship and family slide away as they balance the demands of job, education, and other commitments in their lives. In this paper, we will discuss the significance of keeping up with connections and having a social life, as well as the difficulties that this necessitates and the solutions that can help achieve a healthy balance.

1. **The Importance of Cultivating and Preserving Relationships**
   Wellness in terms of one's emotions
   Maintaining healthy connections with those closest to you is critical to your mental health. They offer a support system that assists individuals in navigating the problems that life throws at them, which in turn reduces stress and promotes mental health.
   Development of Oneself
   Personal development is greatly aided by engagement in meaningful relationships with one's friends, family, and other people in one's life. Learning and growth are both facilitated by engaging in conversations with people about their experiences and points of view.
   Happiness and Satisfaction with One's Life
   A fulfilling and happy life is the product of having a robust social life and meaningful relationships. A person's quality of life can be improved via the joy of shared experiences, celebrations, and support during challenging times.
   Opportunities for Professional Networking
   The opportunity to network can also be found in social connections. Meeting people from different walks of life can open doors to new opportunities for personal and professional development.

2. **The Obstacles That Come With Striking a Balance Between Your Personal Life and Your Social Life**
   Because of Time Restriction
   When juggling job, school, and several other commitments, there is frequently little time left over for social connections. The hectic pace of modern life can make it difficult to keep up with friendships and romantic partnerships.
   Consumption of Energy
   It's possible to wear yourself out mentally and physically if you take on too many obligations at once. When you've had a hard day at work or school, it might be challenging to muster the motivation for social contacts with other people.
   Overcommitting oneself
   It is possible to overlook personal relationships if one is overly committed to their profession or academic goals. It's not uncommon for people to put their professional or academic aspirations ahead of their social life as a priority, which can be detrimental to both.
   Distractions Caused by Technology
   The proliferation of both technology and social media has resulted in the increase of digital distractions, which can impede the development of true social relationships. It's possible that people will spend more time online, to the detriment of their in-person connections.

3. **Methods for Striking a Balance Between Your Personal Relationships and Your Social Life**

Relationships should be given first priority.

Recognize the significance of human connections in your life and make cultivating those connections a top goal. Just like you would schedule time for work or studying, you should also schedule time for your friends and family.

Establish Some Boundaries

Create distinct compartments for your time spent working, studying, and relaxing at home. Try not to bring the stress of your job or schoolwork into your dealings with other people.

Administration of Time

When it comes to juggling several commitments, efficient time management is absolutely necessary. Make sure to stick to your social activity schedule just as religiously as you would a job or school schedule. This will ensure that you get the most out of your time spent with friends.

Digital Detoxification

To reduce the amount of time you spend in front of a screen, you might want to think about participating in a "digital detox." You can improve your ability to be present in your social encounters by reducing the influence that digital distractions have on you.

Tasks can be delegated

When it is appropriate to do so, jobs and responsibilities should be delegated. By working together on chores around the house or delegating responsibilities at work, you can make more time and energy for your social life.

4. **Cultivating and Maintaining Personal Relationships**

Exchange of information

Strong human connections are built on solid foundations of clear and effective communication. Maintaining genuine connections with those you care about requires that you regularly have meaningful interactions with them.

Time Spent Wisely

More important than the total amount of time spent together is the quality of the time spent with loved ones. Make sure that the people you connect with in social settings provide you with an exciting, rewarding, and memorable experience.

Honor the Achievements of the Past

Gather those you care about to celebrate anniversaries, both big and small. Your connections with family and friends are strengthened when you observe significant occasions together.

Show some support.

During difficult times, be there for your friends and family and offer your support. Your ties with those people will strengthen if you are there for them when they are in a time of need.

5. **Maintaining a Healthy Social Life**

Expand your network to include new people.

Participate in a wide array of pursuits and organizations in order to broaden the scope of your social network. Meeting new people can provide opportunity for social development as well as new insights and viewpoints.

Participate in Your Interests

Engage in activities and pursuits that you have an interest in outside of job and school. Join a class, group activity, or sports team that shares your interests in order to broaden your social circle and find others who understand you.

Participate in Social Activities

Take part in social activities such as get-togethers, events, and parties. These events offer wonderful chances to get to know new people and to deepen connections with those already in one's life.

Keep an Open Mind Regarding New Experiences

Be willing to try new things and go on exciting adventures. Leaving the confines of your comfort zone might open the door to enticing new social opportunities as well as personal development.

The demands of employment, education, and other responsibilities can be difficult to manage, but doing so is necessary for leading a life that is both meaningful and well-rounded. Maintaining healthy relationships and an active social life can be difficult, but doing so is crucial. Maintaining personal ties and having an active social life are both essential in today's environment, despite the fact that individuals are frequently pressured to place a higher priority on their employment and academic endeavors. Individuals may strike the appropriate balance and experience the emotional well-being, personal growth, and pleasure that come with keeping an active social life by recognizing the significance of relationships, setting boundaries, and managing their time effectively. This allows individuals to enjoy the benefits that come with fostering connections and maintaining an active social life.

Chapter 10

Future of Cricket and Well-being

Cricket, sometimes known as the "gentleman's game," is one of the most popular sports in the world. It has a long and illustrious history, and its fans are devoted to the sport. Cricket has undergone substantial change over the past few decades, not only as a sport but also in the way it approaches the health and safety of its participants, administrators, and supporters. This essay investigates the future of cricket and how it is connected to the concept of well-being. It covers a variety of topics related to the game, including player mental health, the changing experience of fans, and the role that cricket plays in contributing to the general well-being of society.

1. **The Development of the Cricket**

    Since it was first played, cricket has seen significant development. Multiple facets of cricket have developed over its history, from the earliest forms of the game that were played in England to the global phenomenon that it is now.

    Alterations to the Format

    One of the most important developments in cricket's history has been the game's expansion into a variety of different formats. The sport's popularity has increased across a variety of demographics because to the introduction of shorter formats such as Twenty20 (T20), One Day Internationals (ODIs), and Test cricket. The well-being of players is affected in a variety of ways due to the fact that diverse formats each have their own distinct qualities and difficulties.

    Cricket played by Women

    The visibility and appeal of women's cricket have both increased in recent years. Women's cricket has received increased attention and resources as a result of the proliferation of Twenty20 (T20) leagues and the Women's Twenty20 World Cup. The fact that women's cricket is becoming increasingly popular is a step in the right direction for the diversity and inclusiveness of the sport.

    The practice of business

    The Indian Premier League (IPL) and other Twenty20 leagues have played a significant role in the sport's increasing commercialization, which has had a significant impact on the financial landscape of cricket.

In spite of the fact that this has opened up rich opportunities for players, it has also led to an increase in pressure and scrutiny, which has an adverse effect on player well-being.

Technology as well as Analytical Work

Technology advancements such as Hawkeye, Snickometer, and ball-tracking devices have contributed to improvements in the precision and fairness of decision-making in the sport of cricket. In addition, the incorporation of data analytics and performance measurements into player development and the methods employed by teams has become increasingly commonplace.

2. **The Health and Safety of Cricket Players**

The health and safety of players has emerged as an important component of the game of cricket's long-term prospects. The health and happiness of cricket players can be attributed to a number of different things.

The state of one's mind

In recent years, there has been a significant increase in the amount of attention paid to concerns pertaining to the mental health of cricket players. Players' mental health can be negatively affected by the high-pressure environments, performance expectations, and unrelenting schedules that are common in international cricket. Some of the game's most prominent players, like as Glenn Maxwell and Ben Stokes, have spoken publicly about their challenges, which has sparked a conversation about the importance of mental health support in the sport.

Condition of one's body

Cricket is a sport that places significant demands on the player's body, and injuries are possible in certain positions, such as quick bowling and rigorous fielding. Injury prevention, rehabilitation, and management strategies that work are absolutely necessary for the health and safety of players. Cricket boards have been making steps to monitor player workloads in an effort to avoid players from becoming overworked and suffering injuries.

Fatigue from the Bio-bubble

The COVID-19 pandemic gave rise to the idea of using bio-bubbles as a means of providing protection for both players and personnel. Although bio-bubbles are essential for maintaining public health, they can be mentally and emotionally draining on players because of the isolation from loved ones and the restrictions placed on their movement.

A Timetable That Strikes a Balance

It is essential to have a balanced schedule in order to provide players with sufficient relaxation in between games and series. Constantly packed schedules can cause both physical and mental exhaustion in players, which can have a severe impact on their well-being as well as their performance.

3. **The Experience of the Fans and Their Health**

Another essential component of cricket's bright future is ensuring the health and happiness of its spectators. The cricket authorities and organizers have a responsibility to think about the experience of the fans and how it affects the health of cricket aficionados.

Participation from Fans

Improving the level of fan participation is crucial to cricket's long-term success. Fans are now able to have a more meaningful connection with the sport thanks to the proliferation of interactive technologies, live streaming, and social media. A more satisfying fan experience can be contributed to by providing access to the behind-the-scenes action, fan interactions, and engaging information.

Obtainability of Access

It is essential to the well-being of cricket that it be made more approachable to audiences all around the world. It is helpful to the expansion of the fan base to provide spectators with multiple avenues via which they may follow matches, such as through low-cost streaming services, over-the-air broadcasts, or digital platforms.

Guarding the Fans

It is of the utmost significance to look out for the well-being of spectators at sporting events. In order to protect spectators and ensure that they continue to be healthy, stadiums are required to employ severe security measures.

Both Inclusivity and Diversity are Important

The sport of cricket ought to make an effort to foster an inclusive and diverse fan base. By extending a warm welcome to spectators of all ages, genders, and ethnicities, cricket will continue to be a sport that anybody can participate in, which will contribute to the overall health and happiness of its followers.

4. **The Importance of Cricket in the Fight for a Healthy Lifestyle**

Cricket has the potential to make a significant contribution to the overall health and happiness of not only its players and supporters, but also of society as a whole.

Development from the Ground Up

Putting money into grassroots cricket and getting more kids involved in the game is a great way to encourage physical activity, collaboration, and personal development. Young people can benefit from the development of important life skills that can be gained via participation in sports.

Participation in the Community

Cricket has the potential to engage with local communities by hosting events, coaching clinics, and other social activities in order to connect with fans and address societal concerns. These kinds of activities have the potential to improve people's health and sense of belonging in their communities.

Donations and a Sense of Responsibility to Society

Cricketers and cricket boards frequently participate in charitable activities and projects aimed at promoting social responsibility. These activities have the potential to have a substantial impact on a variety of issues pertaining to well-being, including health, education, and the reduction of poverty.

Motivating Examples to Look Up to

Cricket players, in their capacity as role models, have the power to inspire and positively impact persons, particularly younger generations. Their experiences of overcoming adversity, remaining determined, and attaining success have the power to inspire others to follow their passions and take care of their health.

5. **Obstacles and Things to Take Into Account**

Stigma attached to mental health

Eliminating the negative connotations that are attached to mental health is a continuous struggle. The sport of cricket needs to do more to foster an atmosphere that is both friendly and safe so that players may feel at ease talking about their mental health issues.

Workloads of the Players

The distribution of player workloads remains an area of concern, particularly in leagues such as the Indian Premier League. It should be obvious that there is a pressing need for a thorough scheduling structure to preserve the well-being of players.

Participation from Fans

Continuous efforts are required in order to maintain fan engagement and accessibility. The governing bodies of cricket need to make investments in cutting-edge technologies and platforms in order to improve the fan experience and ensure the fans' continued health.

Access for all

In order to successfully promote inclusiveness and diversity in cricket, both on and off the field, a purposeful and ongoing commitment is required. For the sake of the sport as a whole, it is absolutely necessary to cultivate an atmosphere that is hospitable to all of the spectators and players.

The health and happiness of cricket's players, fans, and society as a whole will have a significant impact on the sport's trajectory going forward. In order for the sport to continue developing and adapting to the requirements of the modern world, it is imperative that it places a priority on the physical and mental well-being of its participants. This includes addressing concerns regarding mental health, physical fitness, and balanced scheduling.

Beyond the confines of the playing field, cricket may play an important part in the overall promotion of health and wellness. It has the capacity to motivate individuals, get people involved in their communities, and make a contribution to important social concerns. Cricket has the potential to continue its growth and to have a beneficial influence on the health and happiness of both individuals and society if it is able to overcome obstacles, embrace inclusion, and cultivate a dedicated fan base. The key to guaranteeing that cricket will have a bright future and that all of its stakeholders will be healthy and happy is to strike a balance between conserving its traditions and embracing new ideas, all the while preserving the spirit of the game.

10.1 Emerging trends in the sport

The realm of sports is one that is always shifting and developing, and as a result, it is constantly witnessing the introduction of new trends that mold the way in which we participate in, watch, and otherwise interact with our favorite activities. As advances are made in areas such as technology, culture, and society, many sports must adjust to keep up with changing standards and requirements. In this essay, we will investigate some of the most significant developing trends in the world of sports.

These trends range from the rise of new sports to the advancement of technology and data analytics. We will also discuss how societal norms are altering.

1. **The Function of Modern Equipment**
   Innovative and Advancing Wearable Technology
   The application of wearable technology in various sporting events is experiencing tremendous expansion. Athletes may now analyze their performance, check their health parameters, and enhance their training regimens with the use of technological equipment such as fitness trackers, smart clothes, and biometric sensors. Wearable technology offers data in real time on the wearer's heart rate, exhaustion, and hydration, which helps in the prevention of injuries and enhancement of performance.

   Both Virtual Reality (VR) and Augmented Reality (AR) are types of mixed reality
   The experience that spectators have at sporting events, as well as the way athletes are trained, is being revolutionized by virtual reality and augmented reality. Athletes are able to prepare and plan their strategies in virtual worlds because to the immersive training simulations that VR provides. By superimposing digital information, statistics, and visual effects over live broadcasts, augmented reality (AR) makes the in-stadium experience more enjoyable for fans and engages them in a new way.

   Electronic sports and video gaming
   The distinction between traditional sports and digital gaming has become more hazy as e-sports have grown in popularity. E-sports contests attract big viewers, which allows professional gamers and teams to gain sponsorships, recognition in the media, and substantial awards. New chances for fans and sports organizations to participate in competitive gaming are made available by the rise of esports.

The Analysis of Data and Monitoring of Performance

The collection and analysis of data as well as the monitoring of performance have become fundamental components of sports. Teams and athletes use sophisticated data analysis to acquire insights on player performance, the techniques employed by opponents, and the best ways to avoid injury. The "Moneyball" revolution in basketball and the usage of tracking devices in soccer are just two examples of how data-driven decisions have become standard practice in sports administration.

2. **Alterations in the Norms of Society**

Both Inclusivity and Diversity are Important

The values of inclusion and diversity are acquiring more and more significance in the sporting world. Roots are being put down for programs that promote gender equality, accessibility, and representation of all people. Athletes coming from all kinds of different origins are rising to prominence, which is challenging existing preconceptions and fostering togetherness in the world of sports.

Psychological Health and Overall Well-Being

The value of a player's mental health and overall wellbeing is becoming more widely acknowledged in the sporting world. Athletes in public positions of prominence have spoken out about their difficulties with mental health, with the goals of decreasing stigma and promoting open discourse. Athletes are receiving support and services pertaining to their mental health from various teams and organizations.

Methods That Are Ecologically Sound

As sporting organizations work toward lessening their negative effects on the environment, sustainability is becoming an increasingly important issue in the industry. Efforts to lessen the environmental impact of transportation, such as lowering carbon emissions and implementing recycling systems at stadiums, are gaining support. For sports organizations, ensuring their long-term viability involves not only a financial but also a moral obligation.

Activism in Society

Athletes are using the platforms they've built for themselves to push for social reform. Athletes have been vocal advocates for causes including racial inequity, the rights of LGBTQ+ people, and the rights of police brutality, which has sparked critical conversations both on and off the field.

3. **The Development of Emerging Sports**

Sports That Push You to the Limit

The popularity of extreme sports such as skateboarding, BMX riding, and parkour has

skyrocketed in recent years. Because these games require a combination of athleticism, imagination, and taking risks, they have a following of passionate participants. They are so widely accepted that they have even been featured in the Olympic Games, which is a reflection of their widespread popularity.

Electronic sports and virtual reality sports

The industry of competitive video gaming, sometimes known as esports, has grown into a worldwide phenomenon, complete with professional leagues, tournaments, and sponsorships. It has established a place in the hearts of spectators alongside more traditional forms of athletic competition. A digital take on more conventional forms of physical activity, such as racing simulators and virtual cycling, can be found in the realm of virtual sports.

4. **Interaction with the Audience**

Interaction via Social Media and Digital Platforms

When it comes to engaging fans, social media channels are essential. Platforms such as Instagram, Twitter, and TikTok are utilized by athletes, teams, and sports organizations in order to engage with their fans, exchange content, and promote upcoming events. The digital sports experience includes things like live-tweeting, behind-the-scenes looks, and interactive polls for fans to participate in.

Experiences Tailored to the Individual

Investing in technologies that tailor the fan experience is something that sports organizations are doing. Mobile apps, customer loyalty programs, and targeted marketing all provide avenues through which sports fans can get curated material and interact with their preferred games in novel ways.

Experiences Based on Augmented Reality (AR) at Stadiums

The usage of augmented reality is bringing about a transformation in the in-stadium experience. During live matches, spectators can utilize augmented reality (AR) apps to get instant replays, player stats, and interactive games. Augmented reality strengthens the link between spectators and the action taking place on the field.

Engagement of Fans Through Virtual Reality (VR)

Fans who are unable to attend live events can still have an immersive experience thanks to virtual reality. Live virtual reality streaming may take viewers inside the arena and give them a comprehensive view of all the activity taking place there. Fan experiences, like as interactive fan zones and post-game celebrations, are another application of VR technology.

5. **Shifts in the Administration of Sports**

The Empowerment of Athletes

The influence that athletes have on the development of their sports is growing. Movements such as the Global Athlete Movement have recently developed with the goal of empowering athletes, advocating on their behalf for the rights they are entitled to, and ensuring that their voices are heard in the decision-making processes of sports organizations.

Accountability and Openness to the Public

There has been a rise in the amount of scrutiny directed at sports organizations, which has led to requests for improved responsibility and transparency. Fair play, anti-corruption measures, and ethical governance are all things that are being demanded in the sporting world by fans, sponsors, and athletes.

6. **Obstacles and Things to Take Into Account**

Concerns Regarding Privacy

Concerns regarding personal privacy are becoming increasingly prevalent as new technologies emerge. The collecting and use of data pertaining to athletes and fans must be carried out in an ethical manner, with due regard for the protection of privacy rights and digital security.

Assistance with Mental Health

Taking on the challenge of addressing concerns regarding athletes' mental health requires an all-encompassing strategy. Athletes need to have access to mental health professionals, and organizations have a responsibility to provide them with the appropriate support and resources.

Commitment to Environmental Stewardship

The genuine commitment to sustainability is required of sports organizations. Greenwashing and other insincere efforts to improve the environment might be harmful to their reputation. It is necessary to take an approach that is both transparent and long-term.

Striking a Balance Between Innovation and Tradition

It is a big task to achieve a healthy equilibrium between upholding the sporting customs that have been passed down for generations and welcoming new ideas. It is essential, when adapting to a changing universe, to respect the roots of the game that you are playing.

The landscape of the future of sports is one that is always shifting and changing because it will be defined by the intersection of technology, societal norms, new sports, and fan participation. The world of sports is undergoing a fundamental change on several fronts, including the incorporation of data analytics and wearable technologies, the expansion of participation opportunities, and the meteoric development of esports.

The health and safety of players, fans, and society as a whole will play a pivotal role in these shifts. It is imperative that privacy, mental health, sustainability, and striking a delicate balance between innovation and tradition be taken into consideration as the sports industry navigates these developments.

In the end, the direction that sports will take in the future will be determined by our collaborative efforts to embrace innovation while preserving the fundamental values and the spirit of competition that have made sports such an important component of our lives. We can assure that sports will continue to inspire, entertain, and positively contribute to our well-being if fans, athletes, and sports organizations collaborate.

10.2 The global perspective on cricket and well-being

Cricket is a sport that was first played in England but has since spread all over the world, transcending national boundaries and cultural norms. It fosters a sense of togetherness and shared purpose by bringing together players and supporters from a variety of backgrounds. This essay will investigate the global view on cricket and its impact on well-being, spanning from player experiences to its function in forging social ties and overcoming cultural boundaries. The world of cricket has been expanding, and in this essay, we will explore the global perspective on cricket and its impact on well-being.

1. **The Reach of Cricket Around the World**
   Competitions held on a global scale
   The fact that there are international cricket championships such as the Cricket World Cup and the ICC T20 World Cup is evidence of the sport's widespread popularity. These events bring together countries from all around the world, fostering a sense of togetherness while also encouraging healthy competition.
   Multiple Kinds of Player Profiles
   The international arena of cricket exhibits a diverse range of player profiles, from West Indian powerhouses like Brian Lara to subcontinental luminaries like Sachin Tendulkar.
   This diversity serves as a wellspring of ideas and brings together fans and athletes from a variety of different backgrounds.
   New Cricketing Powers Around the World
   Emerging cricketing nations such as Afghanistan, Ireland, and Nepal are beginning to establish themselves as major players in the sport. The fact that these countries are allowed to participate in international championships is a reflection of the global nature of the sport and the fact that it has the ability to improve health on a much wider scale.

2. **The Health and Safety of the Cricket Players**
   Assistance with Mental Health
   In recent years, there has been a growing level of worry regarding the health and safety of cricket players at all stages of their careers, from professional to amateur. Mental health issues are now being publicly acknowledged in cricket, and players are urged to seek assistance if they feel they may want it. The worldwide cricket community is coming to the realization that well-being encompasses more than just physical health and that it is necessary to provide care for mental health.
   The Problem That Bio-bubbles Present
   The global COVID-19 pandemic gave rise to the idea of bio-bubbles, which separated participants from the rest of the world in order to guarantee their protection. Even though they are essential, players may struggle with bio-bubbles, which can result in feelings of exhaustion, loneliness, and anxiety. Cricket

organizations are taking action to address the concerns regarding players' health and safety.

Workloads of the Players

Maintaining the health of the players requires ensuring that their responsibilities are evenly distributed. The busy international schedules, particularly for elite players, can lead to exhaustion on both the physical and mental fronts. Adjustments to the schedule and the rotation of players are being made to help offset the effects of these problems.

3. **The Importance of Cricket in the Development of Social Connections**

Crossing International Boundaries

Cricket has the extraordinary capability of reaching across international boundaries and connecting people from all over the world.

In order to celebrate the sport, followers from a variety of nations and cultural backgrounds join together, which ultimately results in the establishment of significant bonds.

Communities of Fans From Around the World

The worldwide cricket community is comprised of more than only the players and authorities of the game; it also comprises fans who are extremely dedicated to cricket. Social media platforms, fan groups, and in-person gatherings all around the world facilitate communication amongst fan communities. For those interested in cricket, participation in these groups can foster a sense of well-being and a sense of belonging.

The Exchanging of Cultures

Cricket encourages cultural exchange by providing both players and fans with opportunities to learn about the traditions and customs of other countries via the medium of the sport. Cricket gives opportunity for cultural study and comprehension, whether it's through the Indian Premier League (IPL), which draws players from around the world, or through travel and films centered on the sport.

4. **The Influence of Cricket on the Health of Young People and Communities**

Improvement of Young People

The sport of cricket is extremely important for the growth of young people. It fosters physical activity, working together with others, self-discipline, and overall personal development. Many countries that play cricket place a priority on youth development programs, which provide opportunity for young players to enhance their skills.

Participation in the Community

Through grass-roots initiatives, coaching clinics, and social activities, cricket actively participates in the communities in which it is played. These initiatives bring wider social issues into the context of cricket and improve well-being in the communities in which it is played.

Motivating Examples to Look Up to

Young people might look to the game of cricket's international stars as a source of motivation and inspiration. Their experiences, accomplishments, and ideals serve as motivation for young people to pursue the things that bring them joy and to live lives that are full. Players frequently interact with younger people through activities like as coaching camps and mentorship.

5. The Problems That Come With Having a Global Perspective

Access for all

Cricket needs to keep working toward its goal of greater diversity. Cricket should make sure that possibilities are available to people of all different kinds of upbringings, and it should continue to be approachable and friendly to people from all kinds of different cultures.

Long-term viability

Due to the sport's international scope, efforts to preserve the environment are necessary. It is imperative that international travel, stadium infrastructure, and resource consumption all be managed with a focus on sustainability in order to lessen the sport's negative impact on the environment.

Respect for Different Cultures

Because of cricket's widespread popularity around the world, it is essential to be sensitive to different cultures. Everyone involved in the game, including players, officials, and fans, has a responsibility to respect the various cultural practices and traditions of the various communities they represent.

In a world that is constantly evolving, the sport of cricket, with its international scope, acts as a unifying factor. The sport is played all over the world, which brings together spectators and participants from a wide variety of backgrounds and helps to create social bonds. It is a very important factor in fostering the health and happiness of athletes, young people, and communities.

Cricket, on the other hand, needs to continue to address difficulties relating to cultural sensitivity, diversity, and sustainability. Cricket has the potential to continue to be a significant cultural phenomenon that contributes to the overall improvement of the lives of individuals who participate in it if these issues are given priority. Cricket's significance in promoting harmony and well-being on a global scale will continue to be a source of inspiration and connection for generations to come, and this is something we should keep in mind as we look to the future.

10.3 Challenges and opportunities for the future

The 21st century has ushered in a period of unparalleled change, presenting society with both difficulties and opportunities that require deliberate thinking and proactive reactions. In order to make the most of these opportunities and overcome the obstacles, humanity will need to respond in a proactive manner. This essay will discuss some of the important issues and opportunities that define our modern period. These challenges and opportunities range from the risks posed by climate change and global pandemics to the potential of advanced technology and the pursuit of social justice.

1. **Environmental Obstacles and Potentials for Improvement**
   Changes in Climate
   The effects of climate change are quickly becoming one of the most serious problems facing humanity at the moment. Ecosystems, people's livelihoods, and the stability of the world are all at danger as a result of rising temperatures, extreme weather events, and environmental degradation.
   Opportunity: The opportunity rests in collective effort to minimize the effects of climate change through international agreements such as the Paris Agreement, shifting to renewable energy sources, and adopting sustainable practices in agriculture, transportation, and industry.
   Loss of Biological Diversity
   The decline of biodiversity poses a significant risk to ecosystems, as well as to the safety of food supplies and the wellbeing of humans. The rate at which species become extinct is speeding up, which threatens the ecological equilibrium of the world.
   Possibility: Efforts made toward conservation, sustainable land management, and responsible
   consumption can all contribute to slow or stop the loss of biodiversity. Educating people, preventing damage to important habitats, and strictly enforcing environmental legislation are all important aspects of the solution.
   Economy Based on Circulation
   The problem is that "take-make-dispose" processes, which are characteristic of a linear economy, lead to the depletion of resources and the accumulation of trash. It is not only harmful to the environment but also wasteful from a financial standpoint.
   chance: Converting to a circular economy, which is one in which items and materials are reused, refurbished, remanufactured, and recycled, provides a chance to cut down on waste, lessen the negative impact on the environment, and develop new types of economic models.

2. **Developments in Technology and the Problems They Pose**
   The Effects of Mechanization on Employment
   The challenge is that machine learning and other forms of artificial intelligence have the potential to eliminate jobs across a wide range of industries, which would result in unemployment and economic upheaval.
   Opportunity: Embracing new forms of technological advancement while simultaneously investing in education and retraining can assist fuel economic growth and contribute to the creation of new job possibilities.
   Privacy and protection of sensitive data

Problem: The advent of digital technology has led to increased worries regarding the safety of personal data, which has resulted in breaches of privacy, cyberattacks, and spying.

Opportunity: The development of stringent data protection rules, cybersecurity measures, and

ethical standards has the potential to improve digital privacy and security while simultaneously assuring responsible data use.

Availability of Information

The digital divide results in unequal access to information and technology. This is a significant challenge. There are still a lot of people who do not have access to the internet or the ability to use technology.

Opportunity: Individuals and communities can be given more power by bridging the digital divide through the provision of inexpensive internet connection, training in digital skills, and the creation of technology that is accessible to all.

3. **Opportunities and Challenges Facing the World's Health System**

An outbreak of a pandemic

The COVID-19 pandemic served to draw attention to the weaknesses of the existing global health infrastructure. New infectious illnesses represent a huge danger to both public health and the stability of the global community.

An opportunity exists to strengthen preparedness and reaction in the event of future pandemics by bolstering public health infrastructure, fostering international cooperation, and developing vaccines.

Diseases that do not spread easily to others

The prevalence of non-communicable diseases such as cancer, diabetes, and heart disease is increasing over the world, putting a burden on healthcare systems as well as economies.

The promotion of better lifestyles through education, preventative treatment, and public health policy has the potential to lessen the impact of diseases that aren't contagious and to improve people's overall well-being.

4. **Obstacles Facing Society and Potential Breakthroughs**

Achieving Social Justice

The problem is that inequalities based on factors such as race, gender, money, and access to opportunities continue to exist in countries all over the world, which results in social unrest and injustice.

Opportunity: Addressing inequities and promoting a society that is fair and inclusive can be accomplished by advocating for social justice through governmental reforms, education, and cultural change.

To educate

The unequal distribution of education that exists around the world as well as within individual nations is a barrier to achieving one's potential and a major contributor to social inequality.

Opportunity: Expanding access to high-quality educational opportunities, particularly in marginalized places, has the potential to give people more agency and to stimulate economic expansion.

Increasingly Older Populations

The effects of an aging population are manifesting themselves in a number of different ways across the globe, including rising healthcare expenses and the possibility of labor force shortages.

Opportunity: Adopting policies and practices that promote healthy aging, learning throughout life, and intergenerational collaboration has the potential to liberate the potential of older individuals and improve societies.

5. **Opportunities and Obstacles in the Economic Environment**

Inequality on the Economic Front

Problem: Economic inequality is a pervasive problem in many countries, and the gaps in wealth and income have reached worrying proportions in recent years.

The implementation of progressive tax policies, the promotion of social entrepreneurship, and the enhancement of labor safeguards are all opportunities that can help reduce economic disparity and support economic stability.

Ecological Economy

Transitioning to a green economy, which places an emphasis on the preservation of the natural environment, can be difficult because of opposition from entrenched interests and a dearth of supporting infrastructure.

Opportunity: Investment in green technologies, sustainable agriculture, and renewable energy can generate new economic opportunities while also decreasing their negative effects on the surrounding environment.

6. **International Politics: Obstacles and Opportunities**

Tensions on the geopolitical front

The challenge is that tensions in geopolitics between major countries, wars in regional areas, and disagreements over resources all pose hazards to the stability of international relations.

Possibility: Diplomacy, peaceful conflict resolution, and multilateral cooperation all have the potential to reduce tensions and foster peaceful resolutions.

Governance on a Global Scale

Problem: The efficacy of global governance institutions, such as the United Nations, has been called into doubt, particularly in regard to their ability to address complicated global problems.

The opportunity lies in the fact that enhancing collective responses to global crises can be made possible by enhancing global governance, reforming international organizations, and encouraging collaboration among nations.

Both the potential and the difficulties presented by the 21st century are extensive and intertwined. The way forward requires international collaboration, innovative solutions, and a commitment to the well-being of individuals as well as societies, whether it be to address climate change, promote social justice, or harness the potential of technological advancements.

Although the obstacles are enormous, the chances for positive change are of an equal or greater significance. Humanity will be able to negotiate the challenging environment of the 21st century and construct a brighter future for generations to come if it embraces a shared vision of a world that is more egalitarian, sustainable, and interconnected.

10.4 The vision of cricket as a tool for well-being

Cricket, sometimes known as the "gentleman's game," has a rich and illustrious history that can be traced back over the course of several centuries. It is a sport that has won the affection of millions of people all around the world, overcoming both geographical and cultural barriers. Cricket has traditionally been linked with competition and athleticism; yet, it is increasingly being recognized as a potent instrument for boosting well-being, both physical and mental. This is because cricket is a combination of team sports and individual sports. Because of this shift in perspective, a new vision of cricket has emerged, one that acknowledges the sport's ability to improve the quality of life for both individuals and communities.

The Contribution of Cricket to One's Physical Fitness:

Cricket is a great cardiovascular exercise because it requires running, which is a fundamental part of the sport. Both the racing between the wickets and the efforts made in the field assist players develop their endurance and keep a healthy heart.

Batting and bowling both involve a high level of strength and coordination, which is beneficial to the development of muscles and an individual's overall level of physical fitness. The game requires the usage of a wide variety of muscle groups, which results in a complete body exercise.

Fielding and diving in order to make catches or stop boundaries are both activities that need flexibility. Participating in cricket on a consistent basis can improve a player's flexibility and make them less likely to sustain an injury.

Interpersonal Communication And Cooperation Cricket is typically played in teams, which encourages interpersonal communication and cooperation. Participation in team sports such as cricket can improve a person's mental health by lowering the intensity of emotions of alienation and loneliness.

The Role of Cricket in Promoting Mental Health:

Concentration and focus are essential for playing cricket, as every aspect of the game requires it, from watching the bowler's deliveries while batting to having to make split-second calls in the field. This focal point has the potential to assist individuals in enhancing their capacity to concentrate in other facets of their lives.

A healthy respite from the pressures and worries of everyday life can be found in a game of cricket, which can help reduce stress. The ability to temporarily escape one's troubles is one of the benefits that it provides to players, along with relaxation and a reduction in tension.

Cricket is a sport that demands players to engage in strategic thinking, problem-solving, and decision-making in order to be successful. Players need to come up with plans to outwit their rivals, which can help improve their ability to find solutions to difficult problems.

Cricket is a game of uncertainty, and players frequently experience challenges and setbacks. Patience and resiliency are necessary traits for cricket players. Conquering these obstacles can help cultivate patience and resilience, both of which are essential for keeping one's mental health in good shape.

Social Support: Individuals who are a part of a cricket team or community have access to a support structure that can assist them in coping with challenges related to their mental health. It fosters a sense of connection and belonging among its users.

The Prospective View of the Future:

The concept of cricket as a means to improve one's well-being is not exclusive to the participants of the game. It affects individuals, communities, and all of society as a whole. Cricket has the potential to serve as a vehicle for developing a sense of community and belonging among individuals of varying skills and demographics through the promotion of social inclusion, diversity, and togetherness.

Cricket for Development (CfD) and Cricket for Social Change (CSC) are two initiatives that have seen significant growth in recent years. Cricket is used in these programs as a vehicle to discuss social concerns such as gender inequity, poverty, and the importance of education. They have shown the ability that sport has in bringing about positive social change and enhancing the wellbeing of populations who have traditionally been marginalized.